BRIDGE MAXIMS

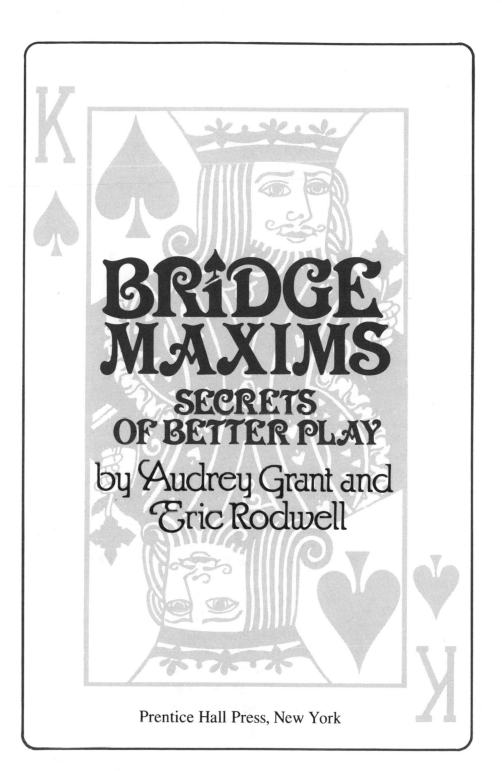

BRIDGE MAXIMS

SECRETS OF BETTER PLAY

by Audrey Grant and Eric Rodwell

Prentice Hall Press, New York

To my son, Jason — Audrey
To my parents, Vic and Meredith — Eric

Published in 1987 by Prentice-Hall Press
A Division of Simon & Schuster, Inc.
Gulf & Western Building
One Gulf & Western Plaza
New York, NY 10023

Originally published by Prentice-Hall Canada, Inc.
PRENTICE-HALL PRESS is a trademark of Simon & Schuster, Inc.

Library of Congress No. 87-60900

I.S.B.N. 0-13-081936-0

Printed and bound in Canada by Gagné Printing Ltd.
10 9 8 7 6 5 4 3 2 1
First Prentice-Hall Press Edition

Contents

Introduction   vii

Acknowledgements   ix

1 Count Your Winners 1

2 Count Your Losers. 23

3 Watch Your Entries 43

4 Watch the Opponents 63

5 Take Your Tricks and Run 84

6 Take Your Losses Early 99

7 Get the Kiddies Off the Street 117

8 Get the Kiddies Off the Street —
The Other Side of the Coin. 135

9 Lead Toward the High Card (The Finesse). 151

10 Lead Toward the High Card —
The Other Side of the Coin. 181

11 Eight Ever, Nine Never 205

12 Eight Ever, Nine Never —
The Other Side of the Coin. 223

Glossary   237

Introduction

Bridge Maxims introduces you to the secrets of the play of the hand—secrets which have been used by the experts for years. Finally, in *Bridge Maxims*, they are put into simple terms that you can use to improve your game.

The sample hands have been carefully selected and tested to reflect the areas that most players, even those who play regularly, need to improve. After reading this book, you will be a better player, regardless of your level of play ... and you and your partners will notice your increased skill. Why? The hands do not reflect unusual or bizarre situations which rarely come up; they represent the hands that you frequently encounter when you sit down for an evening of bridge.

The goal of *Bridge Maxims* is to show you that by using the techniques of the champions ... making a simple plan ... you can unlock the meaning of maxims you have heard from the first time you sat down to play the game, including **draw trump** and **watch your entries**, and understand new maxims, such as **play the high card from the short side**.

A book on the play of the hand is timeless. The truths about playing a hand of bridge are the same now as they were at the game's conception. What is different about *Bridge Maxims*? It is our method of sharing with you the secrets of good play which are used by the best players in the world, in a way that you can quickly understand.

It doesn't matter whether you play a complicated system of bidding or a simple one. The example hands assume that your bidding has taken you to a reasonable spot and you are now faced with bringing home your contract.

Bridge Maxims is a classic book on the play of the hand ... and you are about to see why.

Acknowledgements

We are especially indebted to David Lindop for his tireless help with this project. His ideas were invaluable.

We wish to thank Ted Horning, David King and Paul Thurston for their research and contribution to the construction of the hands.

Connie MacDonald deserves our appreciation for the many hours she spent reviewing and testing the material.

Finally, our thanks go out to the thousands of bridge players and students who have shared with us the areas of the play of the hand that they find difficult and helped us focus on what you want in a book on the play of the hand.

Audrey Grant
Eric Rodwell

1

Count Your Winners

Playing a hand of bridge is like many other endeavors in life. If you look before you leap, or make a plan, you usually increase the chances of achieving your objective. It has been said that you should take care in deciding what you want out of life because, with persistence and luck, you just might get it!

Planning the Play

By following a simple Four-Step Plan for **declarer** play you will be amazed at how quickly and easily your game improves. Let's take a look at the four steps involved in the planning process:

Making a Plan

Step One: *What is my objective?*
Step Two: *What is my current situation?*
Step Three: *What resources do I have?*
Step Four: *How can I use my resources to achieve my objective?*

To translate these general steps into a plan for playing a bridge hand, you need to differentiate between playing in a No Trump contract and playing in a suit contract and restate the steps as follows:

<table>
<tr><td colspan="2">
**Four-Step Plan for Play
in No Trump Contracts**
</td><td>
**Four-Step Plan for Play
in Trump Contracts**
</td></tr>
</table>

Four-Step Plan for Play in No Trump Contracts	Four-Step Plan for Play in Trump Contracts
1. How many winners do I need?	1. How many losers can I afford?
2. How many winners do I have?	2. How many losers do I have?
3. How can I develop extra winners?	3. How can I eliminate losers?
4. How do I put it all together?	4. How do I put it all together?

The difference between the two approaches is that you tend to count **winners** when playing No Trump contracts and **losers** when playing in trump contracts. The final step in both approaches is identical. In this chapter, the first three steps in playing a No Trump contract are discussed. In the next chapter, the first three steps in playing a trump contract are discussed. Chapters Three and Four look at the fourth step in both cases. The remainder of the book shows how to apply these planning steps and make use of the bridge maxims.

Count your winners is an important maxim for declarer. Let's start off by seeing how it applies to the first three steps of planning the play in No Trump contracts.

Step One: *How many winners do I need?*

The answer to this question is clear-cut . . . add six to the level of your final contract. If the final contract is One No Trump, you need seven winners (1 + 6 = 7). If the final contract is Three No Trump, you need nine winners (3 + 6 = 9).

This might seem too simple to be worth your consideration, but it is a part of the planning process that expert players go through with every hand. Before they play the first trick, they have their objective clearly in mind . . . the number of tricks required to make the contract.

Step Two: *How many winners do I have?*

The next step is to see how close you are to achieving your objective. You need to apply the maxim, count your winners. A winner is a card that will take a trick without giving up the lead to the opponents. A winner is also referred to as a **sure trick**.

Before counting winners for an entire hand, look at one suit at a time. You do this by looking at the combined holding in the suit between your (declarer's) hand and the **dummy's** hand. Here are some examples:

DUMMY: ♦ A K Q

DECLARER: ♦ 8 7 3

In this example, you have no winners in your own hand but when you glance across the table at the dummy, you see the Ace, King and Queen. There are three winners in the suit. Since the suit is **evenly distributed**, (there is the same number of cards on each side of the table), it doesn't matter in which order you take the tricks.

DUMMY: ♠ A 8 7

DECLARER: ♠ K Q 3

Here there are also three winners, the Ace, King and Queen. This time, the **high cards** are distributed between declarer's hand and dummy's hand.

DUMMY: ♥ A 7

DECLARER: ♥ K Q

Now you have the same three high cards, but only two winners. You have to follow suit on each trick. On the first trick you could play the King or the Queen from your hand and the Seven from the dummy. On the next trick, however, you would have to put the remaining high card from your hand on dummy's Ace. You cannot win any more than two tricks, because you have only two cards in the suit on either side of the table. In No Trump contracts, you cannot take more tricks than the maximum number of cards you have in either declarer's hand or dummy's hand.

DUMMY: ♣ A 7

DECLARER: ♣ K Q 3

In this example, you can take three tricks with your Ace, King and Queen. Because the suit is divided **unevenly**, with three on one side and two on the other, you have to be careful about the order in which you play these winners. Play the Ace first and play the Three from your hand. Then play the Seven to your two winners. When the cards are divided unevenly, look at the longer side. In this case, declarer has three cards in the suit. That is how many winners you can have. Here is another example:

DUMMY: ♦ A Q 10 8 5

DECLARER: ♦ K J 3

You have all the high cards in the suit. There are three cards in your hand and five cards in the dummy —the dummy has the longer suit. With this combination, you can take five tricks.

Step Three: *How can I develop extra winners?*

Once you know your objective and your current situation, your hand will fall into one of the two categories:

- You have enough winners to make your contract
- You need to develop additional winners to reach your objective

When you have enough winners to make your contract, the play is straightforward. It is pleasant to make your contract by playing Aces and Kings without giving the opponents a chance to take their tricks. Usually, however, there are not enough of these sure tricks and you have to develop extra tricks. Although it requires patience, turning potential losers into winners can be a thrilling experience. The third step in the plan shows how it is done.

There are three general methods that you can use to develop extra tricks when playing in a No Trump contract:

- Promoting cards
- Establishing long suits
- Finessing

Promoting Cards

You do not have a sure winner unless you can take the trick without giving up the lead to the opponents. Consider the following suit:

DUMMY: ♥ 4 3 2

DECLARER: ♥ K Q J

This suit has tremendous potential to win two tricks, but there are no sure tricks even with your powerful holding of King, Queen and Jack. The opponents have the highest card, the Ace. You will have to play the King and give up the lead to the opponents with their Ace. Only then can you enjoy your two winners. By doing so, you will have **promoted** your Queen and Jack. Promoting cards is a solid way of developing extra tricks.

DUMMY: ♠ Q J 10 9

DECLARER: ♠ 7 5 4 2

This suit also has potential to win two tricks, but there are no sure tricks. The opponents have the two highest cards, the Ace and the King. In this example you can promote two of your cards to the position of winners by playing the suit twice. Lead the Queen. You will lose a trick when the Ace (or King) is played, but when you get the lead again, lead the Jack. Even though it will be taken by the opponents, your patience will be rewarded. You have promoted your two remaining Spades, the Ten and Nine, to winners.

When you are defending a contract, you lead the top of touching high cards (a **sequence** headed by an **honor**) to give your partner a description of your holding in the suit. When you are the declarer, since you call the cards from both your hand and the dummy's hand, it doesn't matter which card you play when you have touching high cards. In this book, we'll assume that you play them in order from the highest to the lowest to make the discussion of the hands easier.

> DUMMY: ◆ J 10 9 8
> DECLARER: ◆ 6 5 4 3

Patience is a virtue in this example. You can develop a trick in the suit by promoting your Eight to a winner after the Ace, King and Queen have been played on your Jack, Ten and Nine.

Let's see how promotion works in a complete hand.

Contract: Three No Trump

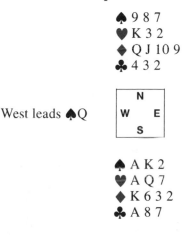

♠ 9 8 7
♥ K 3 2
◆ Q J 10 9
♣ 4 3 2

West leads ♠Q

♠ A K 2
♥ A Q 7
◆ K 6 3 2
♣ A 8 7

Declarer starts to make a plan:

Step One: *How many winners do I need?*

You need nine tricks.

Step Two: *How many winners do I have?*

Spades: 2 (Ace, King)
Hearts: 3 (Ace, King, Queen)
Diamonds: 0
Clubs: 1 (Ace)
Total: 6

Step Three: *How can I develop extra winners?*

> You need nine winners and have six, which is not enough to make Three No Trump. You need to develop three extra tricks. Your only source of additional winners is in the Diamond suit.

You can play the King to drive out the opponents' Ace and establish the three tricks you need through promotion.

Developing extra tricks through promotion is a steady and comfortable way of accumulating extra winners. Now let's look at the second means of developing tricks.

Establishing Long Suits

Consider the following suit:

DUMMY: ♥ 5 4 3 2

DECLARER: ♥ A K 7 6

You have two winners, the Ace and the King. What is the possibility of developing an extra winner in this suit? At first glance, you may think there is no chance. Your small cards are very small indeed. The opponents have the Queen, Jack, Ten, Nine and Eight. But those are the only cards that they have. When you have such a suit, it is tempting to let your imagination run wild. You can visualize that there are more than thirteen cards in the suit, many more, and that your opponents are going to take several tricks if you give up the lead after playing the Ace and the King.

However, when you have eight cards in a suit, the opponents have only five. The good news is that these five cards will usually be divided so that one opponent has three and the other two. Here is an example of how you might expect the suit to be **distributed** around the table:

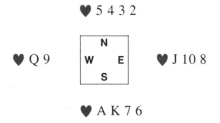

Play your Ace and the Two from dummy. Then play your King and the Three from dummy. Each opponent will have to follow suit. Only one of your opponents will have a card remaining in the suit. If you then play your Seven and the Four from dummy, the opponents will win the trick with their outstanding high card (the Jack in the above example). Even though you have only the Five in the dummy and the Six left in your hand, you will have **established** the Six as a winning trick since the opponents are out of the suit. The next time you have an opportunity to lead, you can take your winner.

When the opponents have five cards in a suit and they are divided as in the above example (three in one hand and two in the other), the declarer refers to it as a **favorable distribution** of the cards. This is referred to as a 3 - 2 **break** or a 3 - 2 **split**; one opponent has three cards and the other two. Although you can hope that the opponents' cards will be divided favorably, there are other possibilities. The distribution could be **unfavorable**. One opponent could have four cards and the other only one—a 4 - 1 break. The distribution could also be extremely unfavorable with all five cards in one opponent's hand—a 5 - 0 break. Let's see what happens when the distribution is unfavorable.

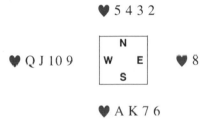

In this example, you cannot **build** any extra tricks in the suit. When you play the Ace, both opponents follow suit. When you play the King, East has no more cards in the suit and will make a **discard**. This is unfavorable. Now if the opponents get the lead they will enjoy two tricks in a suit in which you were hoping to develop an extra trick.

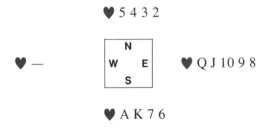

In this example, at least you will know the bad news right away—maybe you can shift your attention to another suit. When you play your Ace, you will notice that West can't follow suit and your wildest imaginings have come to pass ... there are five cards in one hand. We all have days like this, but fortunately, not too many of them!

Let's consider what you can expect in the most common situations. If the opponents have an odd number of cards in a suit, three, five or seven, you can expect them to be divided favorably. If the opponents have an even number of cards in a suit, four, six or eight, you can expect that they will be divided slightly unfavorably. Here is what you can expect:

Number of Outstanding Cards	Most Likely Distribution
3	2 – 1
4	3 – 1
5	3 – 2
6	4 – 2
7	4 – 3
8	5 – 3

Let's put this information to use and consider developing extra winners in your long suits. First we will look at individual suits, then we'll consider how to integrate them into playing the entire hand.

DUMMY: ♥ A K Q J 4 3
DECLARER: ♥ 6 5 2

Here, you have nine cards and the opponents have four. You can expect unfavorable distribution—3 - 1. You don't mind with this suit. You are even prepared to have them break 4 - 0. By playing the Ace, King, Queen and Jack, you will remove all of the opponents' cards and your Four and Three will be winners. You won't even have to give up the lead to establish the suit.

DUMMY: ♠ 8 7 6
DECLARER: ♠ A K 5 3 2

In this example, you have eight cards; the opponents have five, an odd number. You can hope that the distribution is favorable and that the opponents' cards will break 3 - 2. You can play the Ace and the King and then lead the suit again. After you lose a trick, then the last two small cards (with a bit of luck) will be winners and you will end up taking four tricks in this suit.

Even if the suit is divided more unfavorably, 4 - 1, you can develop one extra trick in this suit by giving up two tricks to the opponents. Only if the distribution is very unfavorable, 5 - 0, will you be unable to develop an extra trick. In this case, an opponent will **show out** (discard) when you play the Ace and you will have to switch your attention to another suit.

DUMMY: ♦ 5 3 2

DECLARER: ♦ A 8 7 6 4

Again, you have eight cards and the opponents have five. This time you have to give the lead up twice to enjoy your winners with the **small** cards. Lead the Ace and play the suit again, losing to one of the opponents' high cards. When you get the lead, play the suit again and lose the lead again. After you have played the suit three times, the opponents should be out of the suit—if it breaks 3 - 2—and you will still have two cards left, which will be winners.

DUMMY: ♣ 5 4 3 2

DECLARER: ♣ 9 8 7 6

There is something about a suit with no high cards that makes one want to turn away from it. There are, however, eight cards between the two hands in the above example. The opponents have only five. If there is favorable distribution, 3 - 2, with patience you could develop an extra trick in this suit. You will have to give up three tricks to the opponents. Of course, you will need some winners in your other suits to regain the lead each time you lose it to the opponents!

DUMMY: ♦ A 8 7 6

DECLARER: ♦ K 5 2

In this last example you need good luck to establish an extra trick. You have only seven cards in the suit; the opponents have six. You can expect that the **outstanding** cards will normally be divided 4 - 2. However, you could still hope that they are divided very favorably, 3 - 3. If this is the only place in the whole hand for you to take an extra trick, then you will have to hope for that distribution. Play the Ace and the King and then lead the suit a third time. If this is your lucky day, you will have developed an extra winner!

Treasures can be found in the most unlikely places, so let's look at a hand in which your only hope is to establish a winner in an eight-card suit that has no **honors**.

Contract: Three No Trump

West leads ♥J

```
                    ♠ A 9 6
                    ♥ Q 6 3
                    ♦ A 9 3
                    ♣ 7 6 4 3

  ♠ 10 7 4 3          N           ♠ 8 5 2
  ♥ J 10 9 8                      ♥ 7 4 2
  ♦ J 7 4      W          E       ♦ Q 8 6 5
  ♣ A 10            S             ♣ K Q J

                    ♠ K Q J
                    ♥ A K 5
                    ♦ K 10 2
                    ♣ 9 8 5 2
```

You make your plan:

Step One: *How many winners do I need?*

              You need nine tricks.

Step Two: *How many winners do I have?*

              Spades: 3 (Ace, King, Queen—you have to play your Jack
                            on the same trick as your Ace)
              Hearts: 3 (Ace, King, Queen)
              Diamonds: 2 (Ace, King)
              Clubs: 0
              Total: 8

Step Three: *How can I develop extra winners?*

              You need one more trick. The only hope seems to be the
              eight-card Club suit.

Win the first trick and play a Club, losing it to East's Jack. East will
probably lead another Heart, returning the suit his partner led. You can
win this trick and lead another Club. The opponents will win this trick.
Whatever suit they lead, you can win the trick and lead Clubs again. You
will finally establish a winner in the Club suit, which will become your
ninth trick.

We have looked at two ways to develop extra tricks: through promotion of your high cards and through the establishment of your long suits. In both cases, you need some persistence and patience; you may have to let the opponents win a couple of tricks before you can develop your extra winners.

When establishing your long suits, you also need to hope for favorable distribution of the opponents' cards. Let's take a look at the third method for developing winners. You'll see that you need some luck in this case also.

Finessing

When you try to win a trick with a card that is smaller than a card that the opponents have, it is called a **finesse**. It is another of the common ways to develop an extra trick. Finesses are like building extra tricks with a long suit ... you hope. In the case of the finesse, you are hoping for the **favorable position** of a particular card that is higher than one of yours. Let's look at an example:

DUMMY: ♥ K 3
DECLARER: ♥ 5 2

Suppose you need to develop one more trick to make your contract and this is the only suit which offers some hope. You have the King, the second highest card in the suit. Unfortunately, the opponents have a higher card, the Ace. If you lead your King, one of the opponents will win the trick with the Ace and you will not get any tricks in this suit.

Is there any way you can win a trick with your King? The answer is to try a finesse by leading *toward* your King, instead of leading the King itself. You will have to hope that the Ace is in a favorable position. Let's look at how this gives you a chance to win a trick with your King.

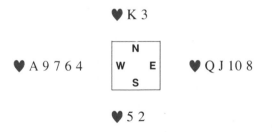

♥ K 3

♥ A 9 7 6 4   N W E S   ♥ Q J 10 8

♥ 5 2

Suppose the cards in the suit are placed this way, with West having the Ace. If you lead a small card from your hand toward the King, West will have to play a card before you need to choose which card to play from dummy. If West plays the Ace, then you play the Three. Your King will take a trick later. If West plays a small card, then you play your King. Since East does not have a higher card, the King will win the trick. Either way, your King has become a winner.

Of course, the opponents' cards may be located in a different manner:

♥ K 3

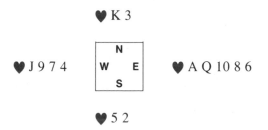

♥ J 9 7 4   ♥ A Q 10 8 6

♥ 5 2

In this case, East has the Ace and there is no way for you to win a trick with your King. When you lead a small card toward the King and West plays a small card, it doesn't matter whether or not you play the King. If you do, East will win the trick with the Ace; if you don't, East will win with a smaller card.

Notice that you are concerned with the favorable location of a specific card, not with a favorable division of the number of the opponents' cards. If West has the Ace, you will win a trick with your King; if East has the Ace, you won't win a trick with your King. This is the essence of a finesse.

Look at this example:

DUMMY: ♦ A Q 7
DECLARER: ♦ 4 2

You have one sure winner, the Ace. However, you might need to develop an additional winner in order to make your contract. Since you are trying to win a trick with the Queen even though the opponents have a higher card, the King, you will have to resort to the finesse. You must hope for a favorable location of the King:

♦ A Q 7

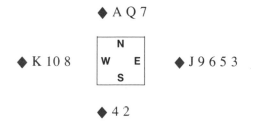

♦ K 10 8   ♦ J 9 6 5 3

♦ 4 2

If this is the layout of the opponents' cards, you can win two tricks by leading from your hand toward dummy's Ace-Queen. If West plays low, you finesse the Queen and it will win the trick because East does not have the King. If West plays the King, you win with the Ace and then play your Queen. Either way you take two tricks.

Of course, the cards may be positioned in this manner:

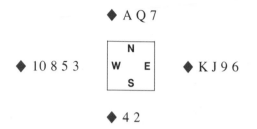

Now, when you try the finesse of the Queen, you will lose the trick to East's King. That's the way it goes! If West has the King, you win; if East has the King, you lose—but that is better than just taking the Ace and giving yourself no chance for a second trick in the suit. Another example: this time the high cards are in your hand rather than the dummy, but the same principles apply.

DUMMY: ♣ 7 5 3
DECLARER: ♣ A Q J

As you saw earlier, you can promote two winners by taking the Ace and leading the Queen to drive out the opponents' King, thereby promoting your Jack. Is there any way to take three tricks? Leading from your hand will limit you to two tricks since, when you play the Ace, the opponents will not play the King, but will use it to take a trick later. However, using the idea of the finesse . . . lead toward the high card . . . you could develop three tricks. Let's see how this works. You will have to hope for a favorable location of the King as in this layout:

If East plays the King when you lead a small card from dummy, you can play your Ace and have both the Queen and the Jack left as winners. What if East plays a small card rather than the King? You will play your Jack (or Queen) and it will win the trick because West does not have the King. Now you are in a similar position to that in our earlier example of a finesse:

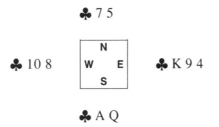

You must return to the dummy and lead toward your hand—assuming that you have a way to get back to the dummy. (See Chapter Three.)

If West had the King, instead of East, you would end up with only two winners. However, two is all you started with, so you have nothing to lose in trying the finesse if you need an extra winner.

By now you can see a pattern emerging. The basic principle of the finesse is to lead toward the card that you hope will win a trick. How does this strategy work in a complete hand?

Contract: One No Trump

West leads ♣K

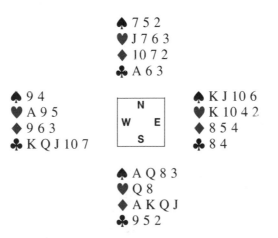

You make your plan:

Step One: *How many winners do I need?*

You need seven tricks.

Step Two: *How many winners do I have?*

Spades: 1 (Ace)
Hearts: 0
Diamonds: 4 (Ace, King, Queen, Jack)
Clubs: 1 (Ace)
Total: 6

Step Three: *How can I develop extra winners?*

You need seven winners and have six, not enough to make your contract. You need to develop one extra trick. Your best potential is in the Spade suit. You may be able to win a trick with the Queen if East has the King.

After winning a trick with the Ace of Clubs, you can lead a small Spade from dummy, planning to finesse the Queen if East plays a small card. In the actual layout, this provides you with the seventh trick you need.

Let's summarize the first three steps of making a plan when you are playing in a No Trump contract:

Step One: *How many winners do I need?* (What is my objective?)

Add six to the level of your contract to determine the number of tricks required to make your contract.

Step Two: *How many winners do I have?* (What is my current situation?)

Add up your sure winners in each suit. Sure winners are cards that can take a trick without giving up the lead.

Step Three: *How can I develop extra winners?* (What resources do I have?)

Examine each suit to determine whether you can get the extra tricks you need by promoting high cards, by establishing long suits, or by finessing.

KEY MAXIM

Count Your Winners

You can tie the first three steps together by remembering the maxim **count your winners**. Before you start to play a No Trump contract, you need to know how many winners you need and how many winners you have. This will draw your attention to the number of extra winners you need to develop and you can start to determine how you are going to get them.

Exercises

1) You are in a contract of Six No Trump. Use the first three steps of the declarer's plan for playing in No Trump contracts to determine how you would play the hand.

♠ A Q 7
♥ K J 4
♦ K Q 9 8
♣ K Q 3

West leads ♣J

```
    N
  W   E
    S
```

♠ K 6 5
♥ A Q 8
♦ J 10 3 2
♣ A 7 4

Solution

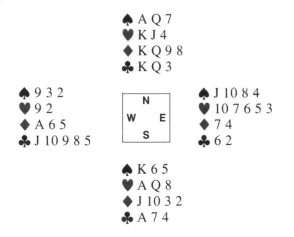

♠ A Q 7
♥ K J 4
♦ K Q 9 8
♣ K Q 3

♠ 9 3 2
♥ 9 2
♦ A 6 5
♣ J 10 9 8 5

♠ J 10 8 4
♥ 10 7 6 5 3
♦ 7 4
♣ 6 2

♠ K 6 5
♥ A Q 8
♦ J 10 3 2
♣ A 7 4

Step One: *How many winners do I need?*

You need twelve tricks.

Step Two: *How many winners do I have?*

Spades: 3 (Ace, King, Queen)
Hearts: 3 (Ace, King, Queen)
Diamonds: 0
Clubs: 3 (Ace, King, Queen)
Total: 9

Step Three: *How can I develop extra winners?*

You need three extra tricks. They can be developed by promoting your high cards in the Diamond suit.

You don't need the first twelve tricks . . . any twelve tricks will do. Win the opening lead with a high Club and then play the King of Diamonds to drive out the opponents' Ace. If they don't take it, continue leading high Diamonds until they do take it. Whatever suit they lead back, you will be able to win the trick and the rest of the tricks are yours.

2) You are in a contract of Three No Trump. Use the first three steps of the declarer's plan for playing in No Trump contracts to determine how you would play the hand.

♠ K Q J 4
♥ Q J 8
♦ A 2
♣ J 5 4 3

	N	
W		E
	S	

West leads ♦ K

♠ A 3 2
♥ A K 5 4
♦ 8 7 6
♣ Q 8 6

Solution

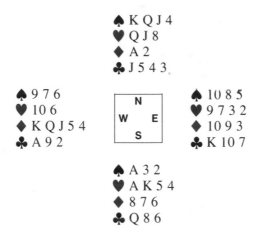

♠ K Q J 4
♥ Q J 8
♦ A 2
♣ J 5 4 3

♠ 9 7 6
♥ 10 6
♦ K Q J 5 4
♣ A 9 2

♠ 10 8 5
♥ 9 7 3 2
♦ 10 9 3
♣ K 10 7

♠ A 3 2
♥ A K 5 4
♦ 8 7 6
♣ Q 8 6

Step One: *How many winners do I need?*

You need nine tricks.

Step Two: *How many winners do I have?*

Spades: 4 (Ace, King, Queen, Jack)
Hearts: 4 (Ace, King, Queen, Jack)
Diamonds: 1 (Ace)
Clubs: 0
Total: 9

Step Three: *How can I develop extra winners?*

In this case, you don't need any extra tricks to make your contract.

Always remember to count your winners. In this example, it seems too good to be true—you have enough to make your contract. Don't turn this good fortune into a problem. Take your nine winners and make your contract.

3) You are in a contract of Three No Trump. Use the first three steps of the declarer's plan for playing in No Trump contracts to determine how you would play the hand.

♠ A 3 2
♥ 9 8 7
♦ A K 7
♣ 5 4 3 2

West least ♠Q

```
    N
  W   E
    S
```

♠ K 6 5
♥ A 6 5
♦ Q 9 3
♣ A K 8 7

Solution

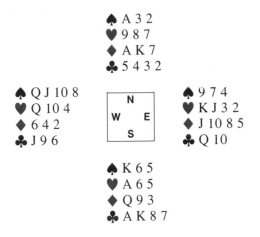

<table>
<tr><td></td><td>♠ A 3 2</td><td></td></tr>
<tr><td></td><td>♥ 9 8 7</td><td></td></tr>
<tr><td></td><td>♦ A K 7</td><td></td></tr>
<tr><td></td><td>♣ 5 4 3 2</td><td></td></tr>
</table>

♠ Q J 10 8		♠ 9 7 4
♥ Q 10 4		♥ K J 3 2
♦ 6 4 2		♦ J 10 8 5
♣ J 9 6		♣ Q 10

♠ K 6 5
♥ A 6 5
♦ Q 9 3
♣ A K 8 7

Step One: *How many winners do I need?*

You need nine tricks.

Step Two: *How many winners do I have?*

Spades: 2 (Ace, King)
Hearts: 1 (Ace)
Diamonds: 3 (Ace, King, Queen)
Clubs: 2 (Ace, King)
Total: 8

Step Three: *How can I develop extra winners?*

You can take advantage of your combined eight-card Club suit and establish an extra trick in your long suit.

Win the first trick and play the Ace, King and then another Club. Since the opponents only have five, you can expect them to be divided 3 - 2. You will lose the third Club trick but will have established your remaining Club as an extra winner.

2

Count Your Losers

Now let's turn our attention to play of the hand in trump contracts. The maxim **count your losers** is an important guideline for declarer, so let's see how it fits into declarer's plan for the play of the hand.

Planning the Play

The Four-Step Plan for playing in a suit contract follows the same pattern as play in No Trump Contracts:

Step One:	*How many losers can I afford?* (What is my objective?)
Step Two:	*How many losers do I have?* (What is my current situation?)
Step Three:	*How can I eliminate losers?* (What resources do I have?)
Step Four:	*How do I put it all together?* (How can I use my resources to achieve my objective?)

The only difference is that the focus is on losers instead of winners. Losers are the tricks you could potentially lose when playing out the hand. In this chapter, you'll see how counting losers focuses your attention on the first three steps of planning the play.

Step One: *How many losers can I afford?*

In suit contracts, consider the objective in terms of the number of tricks you can afford to lose. You need ten tricks to make a contract of Four Spades. The difference between the number of tricks you are trying to take and the total number of tricks available, thirteen, gives the number of losers you can afford: 13 - 10 = 3. You can afford three losers. In Six Hearts, you need twelve tricks and can afford only one loser (13 - 12 = 1).

Step Two: *How many losers do I have?*

Counting losers is an exercise in assessing your current situation. Take a hard look to see how many tricks you could potentially lose if everything goes wrong. This evaluation will focus your attention on how to eliminate the losers you can't afford.

Most players have more difficulty counting losers than counting winners, but once you understand the mechanics, it is easy. The key is to focus on the hand which contains most of the trump, usually declarer's hand. For the sake of convenience, assume that it is always your (declarer's) hand. Look at each suit in your hand in turn to decide how many losers there are.

The losers are the cards which are not sure tricks. Look across the table at the dummy to see if there are any high cards to help out. But don't be concerned about the number of cards in the suit in the dummy, only the high cards. Let's see what this means:

DUMMY: ♥ 5 4 3 2
DECLARER: ♥ A K

In this suit, there are only two cards in your hand, the Ace and the King; both are sure tricks. Even though dummy has four small cards, you are not concerned with dummy's losers, only your own. There are no losers in this suit.

DUMMY: ♥ A K
DECLARER: ♥ 5 4 3 2

This time there are four small cards in your hand. Looking at the dummy, you can see two sure tricks in the suit. That leaves two losers in your hand. It doesn't matter that dummy has no losers; focus on your hand and count two losers in this suit.

DUMMY: ♠ K 9 3
DECLARER: ♠ A 5 2

There are three cards in your hand. You can take one sure trick with your Ace and, looking across the table, you can see the King will take care of one of your small cards. That leaves one loser in the suit.

DUMMY: ♦ J 8 6 3
DECLARER: ♦ 9 5

There are two small cards in your hand. Looking across to dummy, you have no sure tricks to help you out. There are two losers in the suit. It doesn't matter that dummy has four cards; focus on the number of losers in your hand.

DUMMY: ♣ 8 6 5
DECLARER: ♣ K Q J 10

In this case, you don't have any immediate sure tricks so all four cards are losers. However, as you saw in the last chapter, you can promote three sure tricks by driving out the opponents' Ace with your King. You will only lose one trick to the opponents' Ace. You could consider that you have four losers and wait until the next step in your plan . . . How can I eliminate losers? . . . to decide that you will get rid of them through promoting your high cards, but it simplifies matters if you take promotion into account at this point. Otherwise, you may find you have so many losers to consider that you lose track of what you are trying to do. Count only one loser with this holding. Here's a similar example:

DUMMY: ♣ Q 9 4
DECLARER: ♣ K 6

This time you have two cards in your hand. The King by itself is not a sure trick, but looking at the dummy, you can see that your side also has the Queen. You will be able to drive out the opponents' Ace and promote a sure trick for your side. Count only one loser in this case.

DUMMY: ♦ Q 8 6 2
DECLARER: ♦ A K 7 4

Here you have four cards in your hand. The Ace and the King will take care of two of them and, looking at dummy, you can see that the Queen will provide a third sure trick. That leaves you with one loser.

In the previous Chapter, we discussed developing extra winners by establishing long suits. For successful promotion, you usually need a favorable division of the opponents' cards. You expect this favorable distribution when the opponents have an odd number of cards in the suit. In the above example, the opponents have five cards. After you play your Ace, King and Queen, your remaining card will win the trick if the opponents' cards break 3 - 2. This is the distribution you expect. However, it is not guaranteed—the suit might break 4 - 1 or even 5 - 0.

You will not have a loser in the suit if it breaks favorably, but you will if it breaks unfavorably. You might leave this consideration until the third step of your plan—How can I eliminate losers?—but it often simplifies matters to assume that a suit breaks according to the odds. In the above case, there are no losers in the suit, assuming the suit breaks 3 - 2.

Keep in mind that the suit may break unfavorably and later, when you are more familiar with the methods for getting rid of losers, you can start to take this possibility into account as well. Sometimes players give up the valuable exercise of counting losers because it seems too complicated. Simplify it for yourself when you are getting used to the mechanics. Assume the expected distribution (see Chapter 1).

DUMMY: ♥ K 5 2
DECLARER: ♥ A Q 6 4

You have the Ace, King and Queen to take care of three cards in your hand. Count the remaining card as a loser. You have seven cards in the combined hands and the opponents only have six, an even number of cards; the expected break is 4 - 2. You would have to be lucky for the opponents' cards to divide exactly 3 - 3. Assume you have one loser in the above example.

One final example of counting losers in an individual suit:

DUMMY: ♣ 7 5
DECLARER: ♣ K 6 4

You have three cards in your hand and the only high card is the King, not a sure trick by itself. There are no high cards in the dummy to help out so count three losers in this suit. Count possible finesses as losers for the time being because you should have a greater than 50 percent chance of success to overlook a potential loser for the sake of simplicity.

The King might be turned into a winner by trying a finesse (leading toward your King from the dummy), but it is not a sure thing, so for now, consider that you have three losers.

Now let's count losers in a complete hand:

Contract: Four Hearts

♠ 8 6 3
♥ 8 7 6 5
♦ A K Q
♣ K 9 3

West leads ♠K

```
    N
W       E
    S
```

♠ A 5 2
♥ K Q J 10 9
♦ 8 3
♣ A 7 2

You start to make your plan:

Step One: *How many losers can I afford?*

You need to take 10 tricks to make Four Hearts so you can afford three losers (13 - 10 = 3).

Step Two: *How many losers do I have?*

Spades:	2 (You have three cards and only one sure trick.)
Hearts:	1 (You can drive out the Ace and promote all your remaining cards as winners.)
Diamonds:	0 (You have two small cards but dummy's Ace and King will take care of them.)
Clubs:	1 (You have only two sure tricks, so your small card is a potential loser.)
Total:	4

You've now taken a look at the first two steps in declarer's plan. At this point, you will often discover that you have more losers than you can afford. In the above example, you have four losers, but can only afford three. It is time to move on and look at what you can do about the extra loser.

Step Three: *How can I eliminate losers?*

If you have more losers than you can afford, you want to get rid of them. You can eliminate losers by turning them into winners by the same methods as in No Trump contracts: promoting cards, establishing long suits, and finessing. There are two additional methods of getting rid of losers that can be used in trump contracts:

- Discarding losers on extra winners in the dummy
- Trumping losers in the dummy

Let's take a look at each of these methods for eliminating losers.

Discarding Losers on Extra Winners in the Dummy

In some hands that contain more losers than you can afford, you can find some extra winners in dummy. You can discard your losers on dummy's winners. Let's see how this works. In the following hand, concentrate only on the Club and Diamond suits:

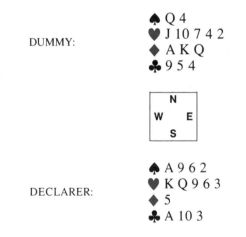

DUMMY:

♠ Q 4
♥ J 10 7 4 2
♦ A K Q
♣ 9 5 4

N
W   E
S

DECLARER:

♠ A 9 6 2
♥ K Q 9 6 3
♦ 5
♣ A 10 3

There are no losers in the Diamond suit. You have one card and dummy has the Ace to take care of it. In the Club suit, there are three cards but only one sure trick. You would count two losers. However, dummy has two extra winners, the King and Queen of Diamonds. Lead your small Diamond to dummy's Ace. Then play the King of Diamonds and discard the Three of Clubs. Play the Queen of Diamonds and discard the Ten of Clubs, eliminating your Club losers.

Let's follow through declarer's plan for playing in a suit contract and see this technique in action.

Contract: Four Spades

West leads ♣K

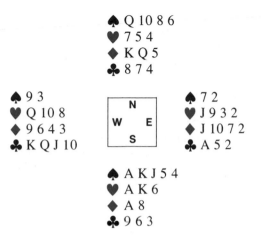

```
              ♠ Q 10 8 6
              ♥ 7 5 4
              ♦ K Q 5
              ♣ 8 7 4

♠ 9 3              N           ♠ 7 2
♥ Q 10 8                       ♥ J 9 3 2
♦ 9 6 4 3     W       E        ♦ J 10 7 2
♣ K Q J 10         S           ♣ A 5 2

              ♠ A K J 5 4
              ♥ A K 6
              ♦ A 8
              ♣ 9 6 3
```

You start to make your plan:

Step One: *How many losers can I afford?*

You need to take 10 tricks to make Four Spades, so you can afford three losers (13 – 10 = 3).

Step Two: *How many losers do I have?*

Spades: 0 (Between you and dummy, you have all the high cards.)

Hearts: 1 (You have two sure tricks, the Ace and the King, leaving you with one loser.)

Diamonds: 0 (You have the Ace and dummy has the King to take care of your small card.)

Clubs: 3 (You have three losers in your hand.)

Total: 4

Step Three: *How can I eliminate losers?*

Since the opponents have led Clubs, it looks as if there is nothing you can do about the three losers in that suit. The opponents will take the first three tricks. However, you can work on the Heart loser. Dummy has a surplus winner, the Queen of Diamonds. This can be used to eliminate the loser.

You plan to play the Ace of Diamonds from your hand and then a small Diamond to the two winners in the dummy. On the third round of Diamonds, you will have none left in your hand and can throw away your Heart loser. You will make the contract since you lose only the first three Club tricks. (In Chapter Seven, we will discuss reasons for playing the trump suit until the opponents have none left (**drawing trump**) before playing the Diamond suit.)

Trumping Losers in the Dummy

Another way to eliminate losers is available when dummy does not have many cards in a suit in which you have losers. You can sometimes use dummy's trump suit to **ruff** (**trump**) your losers. Let's take a look at the mechanics of ruffing losers. Assume that Spades are the trump suit and concentrate on the Heart and Spade suits in the following hand:

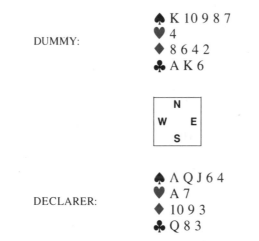

DUMMY:
♠ K 10 9 8 7
♥ 4
♦ 8 6 4 2
♣ A K 6

```
    N
  W   E
    S
```

DECLARER:
♠ A Q J 6 4
♥ A 7
♦ 10 9 3
♣ Q 8 3

There are no losers in the Spade suit, but you have one loser in the Heart suit. However, there is only one Heart in the dummy. After playing your Ace, dummy will have no cards left in the suit. You can lead your loser, the Seven, and put one of dummy's trumps on it. This turns the loser into a winner.

Look for this way of eliminating losers when dummy has a short suit—a **void, singleton** or **doubleton**. Here is an example of how a doubleton in dummy can be used to get rid of one of declarer's losers.

DUMMY:

♠ K 10 9 8 7
♥ 4 3
♦ K 4 2
♣ A K 6

```
    N
  W   E
    S
```

♠ A Q J 6 4
♥ 8 7 2
♦ A 9 3
♣ Q 8 3

DECLARER:

This time there are three losers in the Heart suit. Looking at dummy, there is only a doubleton Heart. This is of no immediate use, but with a little patience, one of the Heart losers can be made to disappear. Declarer (you) will have to lead the suit twice, each time losing the trick to the opponents. Now, dummy will be void in the suit. When you lead your remaining Heart, you can ruff it in dummy.

Let's look at a complete hand:

Contract: Two Hearts

West leads ♠A

♠ J 9 8
♥ Q 10 8 7
♦ 8 7 6 5
♣ A 3

♠ A K Q 4
♥ 5 3
♦ Q J 10
♣ 10 9 6 2

```
    N
  W   E
    S
```

♠ 7 3 2
♥ 4 2
♦ A K 9 2
♣ Q J 5 4

♠ 10 6 5
♥ A K J 9 6
♦ 4 3
♣ K 8 7

You make your plan:

Step One: *How many losers can I afford?*

You need eight tricks to make Two Hearts so you can afford
five losers (13 - 3 = 5).

Step Two: *How many losers do I have?*

Spades: 3
Hearts: 0
Diamonds: 2
Clubs: 1   (Dummy's Ace will take care of one of the
                small cards but you still have one small card
                left.)
Total: 6

Step Three: *How can I eliminate losers?*

You can afford five losers, but you have six. You have to
eliminate one loser. The opponents are likely to take their
three Spade tricks and two Diamond tricks before you win
any tricks. Therefore, you must focus on eliminating the Club
loser. There are no extra winners in dummy on which to
discard it. However, dummy has only a doubleton Club. You
will be able to trump your loser in dummy.

Your plan is to eliminate the Club loser by leading a small Club to
dummy's Ace, a small Club back to your King and finally, your remaining
Club, then ruff it with dummy's trump. (In Chapter Seven we will discuss
drawing trump before playing the Club suit.)

Ruffing losers is an important part of play in trump contracts. It is one of
the advantages of playing in a suit contract since it is a technique not
available in No Trump contracts.

Counting Winners and Losers

Why count winners in a No Trump contract and losers in a trump
contract? While they are two sides of the same coin, the effect of the
trump suit makes it advantageous to consider losers in a suit contract. For
example, the technique of trumping losers in the dummy is not available
in No Trump.

Counting winners in a suit contract would sometimes lead to overlooking
a key point. Look at the following hand:

Contract: Four Hearts

West leads ♣K

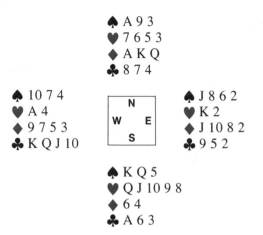

```
              ♠ A 9 3
              ♥ 7 6 5 3
              ♦ A K Q
              ♣ 8 7 4

♠ 10 7 4          N          ♠ J 8 6 2
♥ A 4       W         E      ♥ K 2
♦ 9 7 5 3         S          ♦ J 10 8 2
♣ K Q J 10                   ♣ 9 5 2

              ♠ K Q 5
              ♥ Q J 10 9 8
              ♦ 6 4
              ♣ A 6 3
```

First, consider it from the point of counting winners. You need ten winners and you have seven sure tricks: three Spade tricks, three Diamond tricks and one Club trick. You can develop the extra three tricks you need in the Heart suit by promotion ... drive out the opponents' Ace and King. So it looks straightforward and, after winning the first trick with the Ace of Clubs, you might be tempted to start right away establishing tricks in the Heart suit.

But now let's consider the hand from the point of view of the losers. You can only afford three losers. You have no losers in Spades or Diamonds, but you have two losers in Hearts because you are missing the Ace and King, plus two losers in Clubs. If you lead Hearts first, after winning your Ace of Clubs, the opponents will be quick to take their two Club tricks and you will end up with four losers. This warns you to eliminate a Club loser before establishing your Hearts. You can do this by discarding a small Club on the extra Diamond winner in dummy.

You can count losers in No Trump, but it is not always easy. Consider the following suit:

DUMMY: ♥ K 6 3
DECLARER: ♥ A 7

It is easy to see that you have two winners, but how many losers do you have? In a suit contract, you have no losers because you will be able to trump the suit in your hand if the suit is led after the Ace and King have been played. But in No Trump, there could be many losers left after the

Ace and King have been played. It depends how the remaining cards are divided in the opponents' hands.

Although it is easier to count winners in No Trump, there are times when it is helpful to consider both. Look at the following hand:

Contract: Three No Trump

   West leads ♠Q

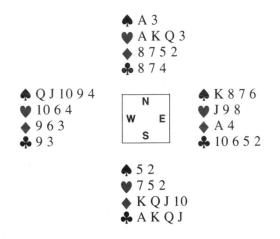

```
                    ♠ A 3
                    ♥ A K Q 3
                    ♦ 8 7 5 2
                    ♣ 8 7 4
   ♠ Q J 10 9 4                      ♠ K 8 7 6
   ♥ 10 6 4          N               ♥ J 9 8
   ♦ 9 6 3        W     E            ♦ A 4
   ♣ 9 3             S               ♣ 10 6 5 2
                    ♠ 5 2
                    ♥ 7 5 2
                    ♦ K Q J 10
                    ♣ A K Q J
```

You need nine tricks and you have eight sure tricks: one Spade trick, three Heart tricks and four Club tricks. Needing only one more trick, you might be tempted to establish the Diamonds by driving out the opponents' Ace. But look what happens! When the opponents win the Diamond Ace, they are in a position to take four Spade tricks as well. They have nine cards, an odd number; expect them to be divided at best 5 – 4. You will have four Spade losers and a Diamond loser. This means you must look elsewhere for your ninth trick.

On this hand, you can hope that the opponents' Hearts are divided 3 – 3 and establish an extra trick through length. You are going to need a little luck since you would expect the Hearts to break 4 – 2 on a normal day. However, once you count the potential losers, you can see that this is your only chance.

Summary

Let's summarize the first three steps of making a plan when you are playing in a suit contract.

Step One: *How many losers can I afford?* (What is my objective?)

Subtract from thirteen the number of tricks you need to make your contract to determine how many losers you can afford.

Step Two: *How many losers do I have?* (What is my current situation?)

Add up your losers in each suit. Losers are cards that are not sure tricks.

Step Three: *How can I eliminate losers?* (What resources do I have?)

In addition to promoting high cards, establishing long suits and finessing, examine each suit to determine whether you can get rid of losers by discarding them on extra winners in the dummy or by ruffing them in the dummy.

KEY MAXIM

Count Your Losers

You can tie the first three steps together by remembering the maxim, count your losers. Before you start to play a trump contract, you need to know how many losers you can afford and how many losers you have. This will draw your attention to the number of losers you need to eliminate and you can start to determine how you are going to do it.

Exercises

1) You are in a contract of Four Spades. Use the maxim, count your losers, to guide you through the first three steps of declarer's plan and determine how you will play the hand.

♠ A J 10 3
♥ A 7 4
♦ 9 8 2
♣ K Q 7

West leads ♥2

N
W   E
S

♠ K Q 9 5 2
♥ 9 5 3
♦ A 7 4
♣ A 3

Solution

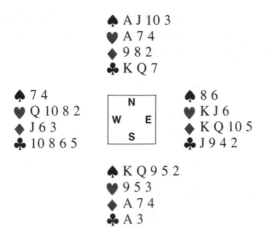

♠ A J 10 3
♥ A 7 4
♦ 9 8 2
♣ K Q 7

♠ 7 4   ♠ 8 6
♥ Q 10 8 2   ♥ K J 6
♦ J 6 3   ♦ K Q 10 5
♣ 10 8 6 5   ♣ J 9 4 2

♠ K Q 9 5 2
♥ 9 5 3
♦ A 7 4
♣ A 3

Step One: *How many losers can I afford?*

You can afford three losers.

Step Two: *How many losers do I have?*

Spades: 0
Hearts: 2
Diamonds: 2
Clubs: 0
Total: 4

Step Three: *How can I eliminate losers?*

You need to eliminate one of your losers. Dummy has an
extra Club winner, so you can discard one of your losers on it.

It doesn't matter which loser you discard on the extra Club winner as long
as you eliminate one of your losers. You plan to play the Ace and the King
of Clubs and then lead the Queen, discarding either a small Diamond or a
small Heart from your hand. (Chapter Seven will discuss playing the
trump suit first.)

2) You are in a contract of Two Hearts. Use the maxim, count your losers, to guide you through the first three steps of declarer's plan and determine how you will play the hand.

♠ K 9 4 2
♥ K 9 7 6
♦ 10 8 3
♣ 7 3

West leads ♣K

```
      N
  W       E
      S
```

♠ A 8
♥ Q J 10 8 5
♦ J 7 4
♣ A 9 4

Solution

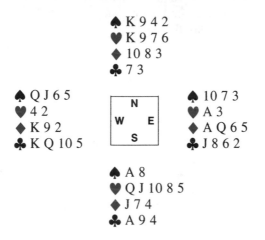

♠ K 9 4 2
♥ K 9 7 6
♦ 10 8 3
♣ 7 3

♠ Q J 6 5
♥ 4 2
♦ K 9 2
♣ K Q 10 5

♠ 10 7 3
♥ A 3
♦ A Q 6 5
♣ J 8 6 2

♠ A 8
♥ Q J 10 8 5
♦ J 7 4
♣ A 9 4

Step One: *How many losers can I afford?*

You can afford five losers.

Step Two: *How many losers do I have?*

Spades: 0
Hearts: 1 (You are only missing the Ace.)
Diamonds: 3
Clubs: 2
Total: 6

Step Three: *How can I eliminate losers?*

You need to eliminate one of your losers. Dummy has only a doubleton Club so you can plan to trump one of your losing Clubs in dummy.

Win the Ace of Clubs and give up a Club trick to the opponents. Dummy will then be void in Clubs. When you regain the lead, you can lead your remaining Club and ruff it with one of dummy's trumps. In the trump suit, you can lead one of your high cards to drive out the opponents' Ace and promote the rest of the suit as winners. (In Chapter Seven we will discuss playing the trump suit first.)

3) You are in a contract of Four Spades. Use the maxim, count your losers, to guide you through the first three steps of declarer's plan and determine how you will play the hand.

♠ 8 7 4 2
♥ 9 7 4
♦ A 8
♣ A Q J 3

West leads ♥A

```
    N
 W     E
    S
```

♠ A K Q J 10
♥ Q 3
♦ 7 5
♣ K 9 6 2

Solution

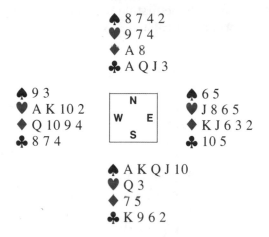

♠ 8 7 4 2
♥ 9 7 4
♦ A 8
♣ A Q J 3

♠ 9 3
♥ A K 10 2
♦ Q 10 9 4
♣ 8 7 4

♠ 6 5
♥ J 8 6 5
♦ K J 6 3 2
♣ 10 5

♠ A K Q J 10
♥ Q 3
♦ 7 5
♣ K 9 6 2

Step One: *How many losers can I afford?*

You can afford three losers.

Step Two: *How many losers do I have?*

Spades: 0
Hearts: 2
Diamonds: 1
Clubs: 0
Total: 3

Step Three: *How can I eliminate losers?*

You don't need to get rid of any losers to make your contract.

Always remember to count your losers. On this hand, you will find that you have no worries. You don't have to eliminate any losers, you can just go ahead and take your tricks. Play the trump suit first so that the opponents cannot trump any of your winners.

3

Watch Your Entries

It is time to consider the fourth step in declarer's plan: How do I put it all together? (How can I use my resources to achieve my objective?)

Thus far, developing extra winners and eliminating extra losers has been discussed one suit at a time. You obtain the extra tricks you need by promoting high cards, establishing your long suits and trying finesses. You eliminate losers by discarding them on winners or by trumping them.

It is easiest to start with the basic principles of obtaining extra tricks one suit at a time. However, the best play in a particular suit may turn out to be undesirable or even impossible when the whole hand is taken into consideration. Have you ever found yourself looking longingly at winners in a suit on the other side of the table, which you can't reach? Have you ever wanted to take a finesse but were in the wrong hand to lead toward the high card? One of the most important considerations when asking how you can put it all together is **entries**.

Entries

What is an entry? An entry is a winner in one hand combined with a card in the opposite hand, referred to as a **link** card, that can be led over to the winner.

The link card is as important as the winner. Look at this example:

DUMMY: ♥ A 4 3
DECLARER: ♥ 2

Here declarer has a winner, the Ace, in dummy and a link card, the Two, in his hand. Declarer can use the Two to get over to the Ace in dummy and so this combination represents an entry. Now consider this suit:

DUMMY: ♣ A 4 3
DECLARER: ♣ –

Again there is a winner in dummy, but this time there is no link card in declarer's hand to lead over to the Ace. Declarer can't use this suit as an entry to the dummy. In fact, if there is no entry to dummy in another suit, the Ace is **stranded**. Maybe the opponents will lead the suit for declarer and allow him an entry to dummy, but even the most pleasant opponents cannot be counted on to be that cooperative!

The value of an entry is more than the value of the winner. It is a way of moving from one side of the table to the other. Why is this so important? An entry can come to the rescue when you develop winners in another suit that could be stranded; it is important for all aspects of trick development. An entry can put you in the right place at the right time.

Using Entries

Entries are used in conjunction with all of declarer's techniques for taking tricks and developing extra tricks through promotion of high cards, suit establishment and finessing. Take a look at this hand:

Contract: Three No Trump

West leads ♣Q

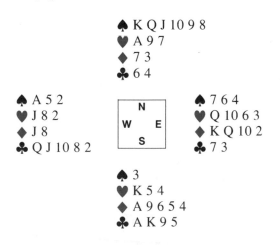

♠ K Q J 10 9 8
♥ A 9 7
♦ 7 3
♣ 6 4

♠ A 5 2
♥ J 8 2
♦ J 8
♣ Q J 10 8 2

♠ 7 6 4
♥ Q 10 6 3
♦ K Q 10 2
♣ 7 3

♠ 3
♥ K 5 4
♦ A 9 6 5 4
♣ A K 9 5

Declarer needs nine tricks and has five sure tricks: two Heart tricks, one Diamond trick and two Club tricks. The extra winners can be developed by promotion in the Spade suit. Once you drive out the opponents' Ace, you will have five extra tricks, more than enough. But what about entries? After the opponents take their Ace of Spades, you will not have a Spade left in your hand as a link card to the dummy. However, the Ace of Hearts is in dummy and you do have some link cards in that suit.

You put it all together by winning the first Club trick and leading a Spade to drive out the opponents' Ace. Even if the opponents don't win the first Spade trick, you can continue leading Spades until they do. Whatever suit the opponents lead next, you can win and use a small Heart as a link card to lead over to dummy's Ace. You can then use the established Spade winners to make the contract.

Here is an example involving the establishment of a long suit:

Contract: One No Trump

West leads ◆ 2

```
                        ♠ A 10 6
                        ♥ 10 9 3
                        ◆ 5 3
                        ♣ 9 7 6 5 3
        ♠ 9 3 2            ┌─────┐        ♠ K Q 7 4
        ♥ K J 7            │  N  │        ♥ Q 5 4 2
        ◆ K J 9 2        W │     │ E      ◆ Q 10 6
        ♣ Q 8 2            │  S  │        ♣ J 10
                          └─────┘
                        ♠ J 8 5
                        ♥ A 8 6
                        ◆ A 8 7 4
                        ♣ A K 4
```

You need seven tricks to make One No Trump. There is one sure trick in Spades, one in Hearts, one in Diamonds and two in Clubs, for a total of five. You need two more tricks. You have eight Clubs in the **combined** hands and the opponents only have five. If the opponents' Clubs are favorably divided, 3 - 2, you can establish two tricks in the suit.

You win the Ace of Diamonds, and play the Ace and the King of Clubs and then another Club. The opponents win the third Club trick and take three Diamond tricks. Since the Clubs are divided 3 - 2, two Club winners have been established. Win whatever they return. You have the Ace of Spades in the dummy and so have an entry to your two Club winners.

Here is an example involving a finesse:

Contract: Four Hearts

West leads ♣K

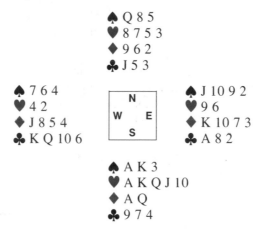

```
              ♠ Q 8 5
              ♥ 8 7 5 3
              ♦ 9 6 2
              ♣ J 5 3
 ♠ 7 6 4                    ♠ J 10 9 2
 ♥ 4 2          N          ♥ 9 6
 ♦ J 8 5 4   W     E       ♦ K 10 7 3
 ♣ K Q 10 6      S          ♣ A 8 2
              ♠ A K 3
              ♥ A K Q J 10
              ♦ A Q
              ♣ 9 7 4
```

Declarer can only afford three losers to make the contract of Four Hearts. You have no losers in Spades and Hearts, but you have a potential loser in Diamonds and three losers in the Club suit. How can you eliminate a loser? There is no hope for the three Club losers. The opponents have led the suit and will probably take the first three tricks. However, there is a possibility of avoiding the Diamond loser by taking a finesse.

You plan to lead a Diamond from the dummy toward your hand. If East plays a low card, declarer can finesse the Queen. Provided that West does not have the King, you will win the trick and no longer have a loser in the Diamond suit.

You must be in the dummy to lead toward your hand. You need an entry. The only card that is available is the Queen of Spades. Because declarer has both the Ace and the King, the Queen is a winner. You have a link card in your hand, the Three, to play over to the Queen. You can then lead a Diamond from the dummy, take the finesse and make your contract.

Entries Within a Suit

When the cards are evenly divided between the dummy and declarer's hand, entries are not a problem.

DUMMY: ♠ A K Q 8 2
DECLARER: ♠ J 10 7 6 4

In this example, since there are five cards in the dummy and five cards in declarer's hand, the suit can be played in any order. The suit will run out on both sides of the table at the same time.

DUMMY: ♥ A Q 3

DECLARER: ♥ K 7 6

Here, again, there is no problem with entries between the two hands. There are three winners and, with the same number of cards on each side of the table, the declarer can take these winners in any order. This type of suit, a short suit with no chance for extra tricks, it is often useful for providing entries for other suits. There are two entries to the dummy, the Ace and the Queen, and one entry to declarer's hand, the King.

Look at what happens when the cards are unevenly divided between dummy and declarer:

DUMMY: ♦ A Q J 10 2

DECLARER: ♦ K 3

If there are no entries to the dummy in another suit, the **order** in which declarer plays the cards in the suit is very important.

Suppose you play dummy's Ace first and the Three from your own hand. Now you lead the Two from dummy over to the King in your hand. The Queen, Jack and Ten are all winners, but they are stranded in the dummy. You have no link card left in your hand to reach them.

There is a simple solution to this dilemma: change the order in which the cards are played. Win the first trick with the King in your hand, playing the Two from dummy. Now you can use the Three as a link card over to the dummy and take the remaining winners.

DUMMY: ♥ A K 4

DECLARER: ♥ Q 7

In this example, if you play the dummy's Ace first then the Seven from your hand, followed by the Four from dummy to the Queen in your hand, the King will be stranded in the dummy. Instead, you must play the Four from dummy to the Queen; then play the Seven back over to the two winners in the dummy.

It's time for a maxim that will guide you to the most efficient way to take winners in a suit that is unevenly divided between the two hands: **play the high card from the short side.**

Entries are a problem when a suit is unevenly divided—with more cards on one side than the other—even when you have all of the high cards. This maxim reminds you that, when you are taking winners, start by playing the winners in the hand with the fewer cards—the short side.

Let's look at an example in a complete hand:

Contract: Four Spades

West leads the ♥K

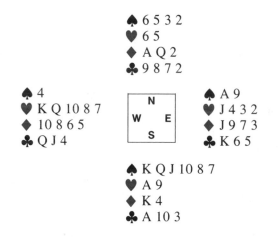

Declarer can afford only three losers. There are four potential losers: one in the Spade suit, one in Hearts, none in Diamonds, two in Clubs. You must eliminate one of the losers. Dummy has the Queen of Diamonds, an extra winner, and you can make use of this to discard a loser.

You must be careful because there is no entry to the dummy outside of the Diamond suit itself. The suit is unevenly divided so you must start by playing the high card from the short side. This means playing the King of Diamonds first and then playing the Four over to the two winners in the dummy. On the third Diamond trick, you can discard one of your losers.

Playing the high card from the short side also applies when declarer is trying to promote tricks by driving out the opponents' high cards in a suit that is unevenly divided between the two hands:

DUMMY: ♠ K J 10 9 4

DECLARER: ♠ Q 5

You want to establish four winners in this suit by driving out the Ace. There is another high card in the dummy, the Ace of Clubs. If you play a high Spade and the opponents play the Ace to win the trick, there is no problem. Your suit is set up and you have the Ace of Clubs to get to the winners.

We are going to assume that the opponents make things more difficult for you by not playing their Ace right away. First, look what happens if the declarer does not play the high card from the short side. The first trick is won with a high card in dummy. The second trick is won with the Queen in declarer's hand ... two easy tricks. Declarer has no link card to lead Spades again. You have to use the Ace of Clubs to get to dummy to play a third round of Spades. Finally, the opponents play the Ace. You have two good Spades in dummy, but they are stranded since the Ace of Clubs needed to be used to play the third round of Spades.

Look how efficiently the suit develops if you win the first trick with the high card, the Queen of Spades, in your hand. Next, lead a low Spade over to one of dummy's winners. You are now in the dummy and can play Spades the third time. The opponents play the Ace. When you get the lead back, you have two Spade winners in the dummy and a way to get to them with the Ace of Clubs.

Let's see how this works in a complete hand:

Contract: Three No Trump

West leads ♠7

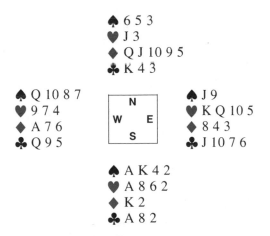

Declarer needs nine tricks to make the contract. There are five sure winners: the Ace and the King of Spades, the Ace of Hearts, and the Ace and the King of Clubs. To develop the extra winners, declarer plans to promote four tricks in the Diamond suit by driving out the opponents' Ace.

After winning the first trick, you lead the King of Diamonds, playing the high card from the short side in the suit you want to establish. If the opponents don't take their Ace right away, you can continue by playing your link card, the Two, over to the Diamonds in dummy and continue leading them until the Ace is **driven out**. When you regain the lead, you can use dummy's King of Clubs as an entry to the established winners.

If you played the Diamond Two first and then led dummy's Five back to your own King, you would be in trouble if the opponents did not take their Ace. You could use the King of Clubs as an entry to get to dummy and continue leading the suit to drive out the Ace, but the remaining winners would be stranded because dummy has no more entries.

You don't always play the high card from the short hand when a suit is unevenly divided. Consider the following suit:

DUMMY: ♠ A 8 7
DECLARER: ♠ K 4

Although the suit is unevenly divided, it doesn't matter which card you win first within the suit itself. There are only two high cards in the suit, the Ace and the King. Since there are two cards on the shorter side, the declarer's side, there will be a link card for both of these winners. This suit is best used to provide the entry cards you need to build tricks in other suits. Use the suit wisely. Since the first trick in this suit could be won by dummy or declarer, decide where you would like to be. Where you win the first trick with such suits can be the difference between making your contract and going down. Let's see how this concept can be useful in planning the play of a complete hand:

Contract: Three No Trump

West leads ♥Q

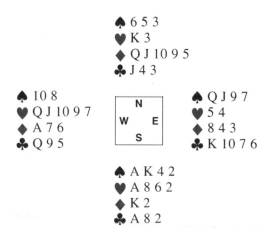

This hand is similar to the previous one. Declarer needs nine tricks and starts with five sure tricks: the Ace and the King of Spades, the Ace and the King of Hearts, and the Ace of Clubs. Declarer will have to establish the Diamond suit to obtain the extra winners needed to make the contract.

The Queen of Hearts has been led. If you blindly follow the maxim and win the trick in the short hand first, with dummy's King, you may not make the contract. When you try to promote the Diamond suit by playing a Diamond to the King, West may not take the Ace. If you continue to lead the suit, West can win the trick and dummy's remaining Diamond winners are stranded. There is no entry left.

You must realize that you are not planning to take more than two tricks in the Heart suit. You can use the Ace and the King as entries for other suits. Realizing that you may need an entry to the dummy, you keep the King in the dummy as long as possible and win the first trick in your hand with the Ace. You will thus preserve the King as an entry to the dummy when you have established the Diamond winners.

In addition to playing the high card from the short side first, there is another way to preserve entries within an unevenly divided suit that you are trying to establish. Take a look at this example:

DUMMY: ♥ A K 8 6 3 2

DECLARER: ♥ 7 5

If there are no entries to the dummy in another suit, the order in which declarer plays these cards can make a difference. The normal way to develop winners in this suit is to play the Ace and the King and lead the suit a third time. If the opponents' cards are divided 3 – 2, the remaining three cards will be winners. However, if there is no entry to the dummy in another suit, the winners will be stranded.

To avoid this situation, you need to alter the order of play slightly. Instead of winning the first two tricks and losing the third trick, declarer should *lose* the first trick. This leaves declarer with a link card to play to dummy and take the Ace and the King. Now, you will be in the dummy when the suit is established and can play the rest of your winners.

It is difficult to concede a trick to the opponents when you could win the trick instead. You want to maintain a warm relationship with your partner, and you might worry what your partner will think of your losing a trick in the suit when you have both the Ace and the King in dummy. You may be concerned about letting the opponents win a trick, because they might do something horrid, like take the rest of the tricks! Yet unless you plan to take all of the tricks every time you play a contract, you have to become used to letting the opponents **take the lead** several times in each hand. It is important to understand that you can often **control** when they have the lead. **Timing** is everything—and with planning, you can decide when to give your opponents the lead. As a general rule, don't be afraid to let the opponents have their tricks early on in the game.

Deliberately losing a trick to the opponents is called **ducking** and you can keep this technique in mind with the maxim **duck to preserve an entry.**

Let's see how this can be useful in a complete hand.

Contract: Three No Trump

West leads ♥Q

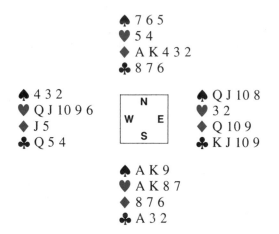

```
                    ♠ 7 6 5
                    ♥ 5 4
                    ♦ A K 4 3 2
                    ♣ 8 7 6

    ♠ 4 3 2                      ♠ Q J 10 8
    ♥ Q J 10 9 6      N          ♥ 3 2
    ♦ J 5          W     E       ♦ Q 10 9
    ♣ Q 5 4           S          ♣ K J 10 9

                    ♠ A K 9
                    ♥ A K 8 7
                    ♦ 8 7 6
                    ♣ A 3 2
```

You need nine tricks to reach your goal. You have seven winners: two Spades, two Hearts, two Diamonds and one Club. The best source for extra tricks is in the Diamond suit. Declarer can establish two additional tricks if the opponents' cards divide favorably, 3 – 2.

Since the cards are unevenly divided between the two hands, declarer has to be careful not to strand the winners in the dummy. Is there an entry in the dummy other than in the Diamond suit? No. Therefore, the Diamond suit will have to provide its own entry. The maxim, duck to preserve an entry, provides the method. After winning the opening lead, you lead a Diamond from your hand and play a low Diamond from the dummy. The opponents will win the trick. However, whatever suit the opponents lead, you can win the trick, and now the Diamonds are ready to go. You lead another Diamond from your hand to dummy's Ace and then play the

King, removing the opponents' remaining Diamond. Now the two small Diamonds in dummy are winners and declarer is in the right place at the right time.

Creating an Entry

Sometimes you need an entry, but there is no obvious entry available. In this case, you might have to manufacture one. Take a look at the following hand:

Contract: Three No Trump

West leads ♠Q

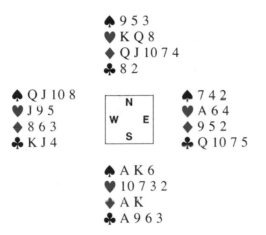

You need nine tricks. You have eight sure tricks: the Ace and the King of Spades; the Ace, King, Queen, Jack and Ten of Diamonds, the Ace of Clubs. You will need one additional trick, which can come from the Heart suit. You can use your King to drive out the opponents' Ace and promote your Queen into a winner.

However, there is a problem. After taking your Ace and King of Diamonds, you have no link card to get to dummy's remaining Diamond winners. You will need an entry in another suit. There is no ready entry available, but you can create one in the Heart suit. When you have driven out the Ace with your King, the Queen will have been promoted into a winner and can serve as an entry to the dummy.

You must be careful about the order in which you play the cards. After winning the first Spade trick, take the Ace and the King of Diamonds.

Next, lead a Heart to dummy's King to drive out the Ace. If the opponents win the trick with their Ace, your Queen will be an entry to the Diamonds. If the opponents do not win the Ace, your King will win the trick and you will be in the dummy and can take your three Diamond winners. Either way, you will make your contract: two Spade tricks, one Heart trick, five Diamond tricks, and one Club trick.

In the last case, you could create a sure entry to dummy. Sometimes, the situation is a little more doubtful.

Contract: Three No Trump

West leads ♥J

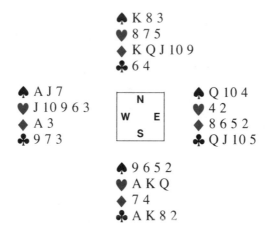

♠ K 8 3
♥ 8 7 5
♦ K Q J 10 9
♣ 6 4

♠ A J 7
♥ J 10 9 6 3
♦ A 3
♣ 9 7 3

♠ Q 10 4
♥ 4 2
♦ 8 6 5 2
♣ Q J 10 5

♠ 9 6 5 2
♥ A K Q
♦ 7 4
♣ A K 8 2

Again, you need nine winners and start with five: three Heart tricks and two Club tricks. You need four extra winners and Diamonds are the obvious choice. You plan to drive out the Ace and promote your remaining cards into winners. But you will have a problem if the opponents do not win the first Diamond trick. If they win the second Diamond trick with their Ace, you will have no Diamonds left as a link to dummy.

You will need an entry in another suit. The only possibility is dummy's King of Spades. After establishing the Diamond tricks, you can take a finesse by leading a small Spade toward the King.

If West has the Ace, your Spade King will become the entry you need. If East has the Ace, you will be out of luck. Whether or not you make your contract will depend on the location of the Ace of Spades.

Here is a dramatic example in which you have to be quite creative to manufacture an entry.

Contract: Three No Trump

West leads ♠7

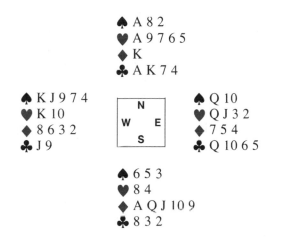

              ♠ A 8 2
              ♥ A 9 7 6 5
              ♦ K
              ♣ A K 7 4

♠ K J 9 7 4   ♠ Q 10
♥ K 10   ♥ Q J 3 2
♦ 8 6 3 2   ♦ 7 5 4
♣ J 9   ♣ Q 10 6 5

              ♠ 6 5 3
              ♥ 8 4
              ♦ A Q J 10 9
              ♣ 8 3 2

You need nine tricks and you appear to have them: one Spade, the Ace; one Heart, the Ace; five Diamonds, the Ace, King, Queen, Jack and Ten; two Clubs, the Ace and the King. However, when you try to put it all together, there is a problem. There is no outside entry to your hand. If you win the Ace of Spades and play the King of Diamonds, taking the high card from the short side, there is no link card left in the dummy to get to the rest of the Diamond winners in your hand.

The only way around this problem is to use the King of Diamonds as the link card! When you lead the King, instead of playing the Nine from your hand, you must **overtake** it with the Ace. Now, you will be in your hand and can take the rest of the Diamond winners. You didn't lose a King; you gained an Ace, Queen, Jack, Ten and Nine.

Watching your entries is an important part of declarer's plan when putting it all together.

Summary

Now you are ready to put all four steps of declarer's plan into action:

Four-Step Plan for Play in No Trump Contracts	Four Step Plan For Play in Trump Contracts
1. How many winners do I need?	1. How many losers can I afford?
2. How many winners do I have?	2. How many losers do I have?
3. How can I develop extra winners?	3. How can I eliminate losers?
4. How do I put it all together?	4. How do I put it all together?

After you have taken a look at your sources of extra winners or for eliminating losers in the third step, you need to put it all together by considering the hand as a whole. In doing this, you must consider your entries between the two hands.

KEY MAXIM

Watch Your Entries

In watching your entries, you must be careful to keep the following maxims in mind: **Play the high card from the short side** and **duck to preserve an entry.**

Exercises

1) You are in a contract of Two Spades. Use the maxim, watch your entries, to guide you through all four steps of declarer's plan to determine how you will play the hand.

♠ 6 5 3 2
♥ A K 3
♦ J 8 2
♣ 4 3 2

West leads ♦K

```
    N
 W     E
    S
```

♠ Q J 10 9 8
♥ Q 5
♦ 9 7 4
♣ A K 6

Solution

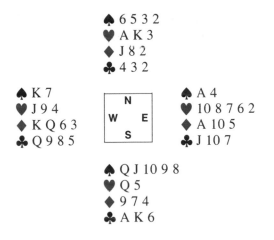

♠ 6 5 3 2
♥ A K 3
♦ J 8 2
♣ 4 3 2

♠ K 7
♥ J 9 4
♦ K Q 6 3
♣ Q 9 8 5

♠ A 4
♥ 10 8 7 6 2
♦ A 10 5
♣ J 10 7

♠ Q J 10 9 8
♥ Q 5
♦ 9 7 4
♣ A K 6

Step One: *How many losers can I afford?*

You can afford 5 losers (13 – 8 = 5).

Step Two: *How many losers do I have?*

Spades: 2
Hearts: 0
Diamonds: 3
Clubs: 1
Total: 6

Step Three: *How can I eliminate losers?*

There is not much you can do about the Diamonds. The opponents have led them and will take the first three tricks. You also can't do anything about the Ace and the King of trumps. You will have to get rid of the Club loser. You can do this by discarding it on the extra Heart winner in dummy.

Step Four: *How do I put it all together?*

You will have to watch your entries in the Heart suit. Play the high card from the short side, your Queen, first. Then you can use the Five as a link card to dummy's Ace. Now, you can play the dummy's King and discard your Club loser.

2) You are in a contract of One No Trump. Use the maxim, watch your
entries, to guide you through all four steps of declarer's plan to
determine how you will play the hand.

$$\spadesuit\ 6\ 5\ 2$$
$$\heartsuit\ J\ 2$$
$$\diamondsuit\ A\ 7\ 6\ 5\ 2$$
$$\clubsuit\ 6\ 5\ 4$$

West leads ♠Q

N
W   E
S

$$\spadesuit\ A\ K\ 3$$
$$\heartsuit\ A\ 4\ 3$$
$$\diamondsuit\ K\ 4\ 3$$
$$\clubsuit\ Q\ 9\ 8\ 7$$

Solution

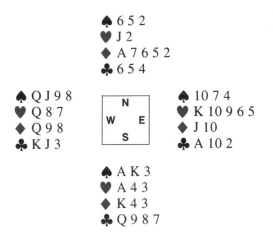

♠ 6 5 2
♥ J 2
♦ A 7 6 5 2
♣ 6 5 4

♠ Q J 9 8
♥ Q 8 7
♦ Q 9 8
♣ K J 3

♠ 10 7 4
♥ K 10 9 6 5
♦ J 10
♣ A 10 2

♠ A K 3
♥ A 4 3
♦ K 4 3
♣ Q 9 8 7

Step One: *How many winners do I need?*

You need 7 tricks.

Step Two: *How many winners do I have?*

Spades: 2
Hearts: 1
Diamonds: 2
Clubs: 0
Total: 5

Step Three: *How can I develop extra winners?*

Because you have eight cards in the Diamond suit, it offers the best chance to develop the two extra winners you need. By playing the Ace and the King, and giving up a trick to the opponents, you can establish the remaining Diamonds as winners if the suit breaks 3 – 2.

Step Four: *How do I put it all together?*

You must watch your entries. There are no entries to dummy outside the Diamond suit. Since the Diamonds are unevenly divided, you can use the maxim, duck to preserve an entry. After winning the first Spade trick, play a small Diamond from your hand and a small Diamond from dummy. You can win whatever suit the opponents play and now you can take your Diamond tricks by playing the King and your remaining small Diamond to dummy's Ace. You will be in the dummy to take your two established winners.

3) You are in a contract of Four Spades. Use the maxim, watch your entries, to guide you through the four steps of declarer's plan to determine how you will play the hand.

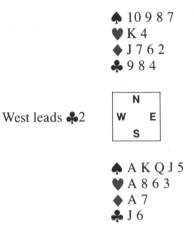

♠ 10 9 8 7
♥ K 4
♦ J 7 6 2
♣ 9 8 4

West leads ♣2

♠ A K Q J 5
♥ A 8 6 3
♦ A 7
♣ J 6

Solution

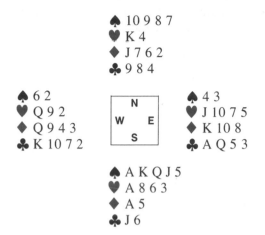

♠ 10 9 8 7
♥ K 4
♦ J 7 6 2
♣ 9 8 4

♠ 6 2
♥ Q 9 2
♦ Q 9 4 3
♣ K 10 7 2

♠ 4 3
♥ J 10 7 5
♦ K 10 8
♣ A Q 5 3

♠ A K Q J 5
♥ A 8 6 3
♦ A 5
♣ J 6

Step One: *How many losers can I afford?*

You can lose 3 tricks (13 – 10 = 3).

Step Two: *How many losers do I have?*

Spades: 0
Hearts: 2
Diamonds: 1
Clubs: 2
Total: 5

Step Three: *How can I eliminate losers?*

You can't do anything about the two Club losers and there is nowhere to discard the Diamond loser. However, dummy has only two Hearts, so you can plan to trump your Heart losers in dummy.

Step Four: *How do I put it all together?*

Plan your entries carefully when eliminating your Heart losers. You should plan to play a Heart to dummy's King first (high card from the short side) and then a Heart back to your Ace. You will then be in your hand and can lead one of your small Hearts and trump it in dummy. You will now need an entry back to your hand so that you can lead your last Heart and trump it in dummy. You can use either the Diamond Ace (if you have not already played it) or one of the trump tricks in your hand.

4

Watch the Opponents

Up to this point, we have not presented the opponents as much of a threat. When they led a suit in No Trump, you had enough high cards to stop them from taking too many tricks and when they led against a trump contract, you were able to trump their winners.

But while you are planning ways of developing extra tricks and eliminating losers, the opponents are making their own plans. The opponents try to do two things:

- Establish and take their tricks
- Stop you from taking your tricks

When you come to the fourth step of your plan—how do I put it all together?—you need to consider what the opponents might do to interfere with your plan.

The opponents have the advantage of making the **opening lead**. They can start establishing and taking their tricks before you get an opportunity to develop your tricks. Let's start off by considering one of the tactics you can employ to prevent the opponents from taking their tricks.

The Hold-up Play

In a suit contract, you can usually prevent the opponents from taking too many tricks in their suit by using your trump cards to ruff their winners once you have no cards left in the suit. In No Trump, you have to depend on your high card strength, and your timing, to prevent the opponents from running their suit. You can sometimes extend the value of your high cards by playing them on the right trick at the right time.

Here is another saying you might have heard: **hold up your Ace**. It is a reminder that you shouldn't always take your Ace right away; sometimes it is better to wait for the right moment. Consider the following **layout** of the Heart suit:

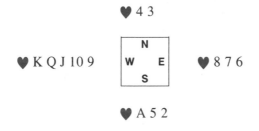

West leads the King of Hearts against your No Trump contract. You have only one winner in the suit, the Ace. Timing, that is, choosing when to take your Ace, can make a crucial difference. Suppose you win the first trick with your Ace. This is what is left of the suit:

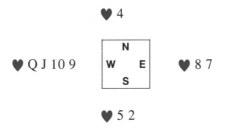

West has promoted four winning Heart tricks now that the Ace is gone. Unless you immediately have enough sure winners to make your contract, you may have to give up a trick to the opponents to develop additional winners. When they get another opportunity to lead, they will be able to take their Heart winners. If East gets the lead, he has a link card to get to West's winners, and West will take four tricks. Let's look at the example again and see what happens when you hold up your Ace.

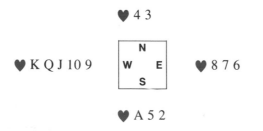

You let the opponents win the first two Heart tricks and you win the third trick with your Ace. Now the remaining cards in the suit look like this:

♥ –

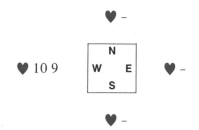

♥ 10 9   ♥ –

♥ –

What a difference timing makes! The only player who has any Hearts left is West. These two cards are winners . . . if he can get on lead to play them. Unless West has a high card in another suit to serve as an entry, the winners are stranded. By holding up, that is, by not playing your winner until the third round, you have ensured that East has no link card left to West's winners. If you have to give up a trick and East wins it, he cannot lead a Heart. Played at the right time, declarer's Ace is more than just a card that can take one trick. So remember to hold up your Ace.

The magic of the **hold-up play** can be seen in the following hand:

Contract: Three No Trump

West leads ♠K

```
              ♠ 8 3
              ♥ Q 10 9
              ♦ K J 10 5
              ♣ A J 7 3

♠ K Q J 10 4        N        ♠ 6 5 2
♥ K 8 6                      ♥ J 7 3 2
♦ 9 6 3        W     E       ♦ A 8 2
♣ 10 8              S        ♣ 9 6 5

              ♠ A 9 7
              ♥ A 5 4
              ♦ Q 7 4
              ♣ K Q 4 2
```

Declarer's goal is to take nine tricks. You have one sure trick in Spades, one in Hearts, none in Diamonds and four in Clubs, for a total of six. You need three more winners. These winners can easily be promoted in the Diamond suit—after the opponents' Ace has been driven out.

The problem with this hand lies with the opponents. As soon as they obtain the lead, they can take their winners. You can try to protect yourself on this hand by using the hold-up play.

Let the opponents have the first two Spade tricks. When they lead Spades for the third time, play the Ace. Now go after your Diamonds by playing the Queen, the high card from the short side. East has the Ace. When he wins the trick he cannot return a Spade because he has no link cards left. He will have to return a Heart, Diamond or Club and you can win this lead and take the rest of your tricks.

On this hand, the Spades were divided 5-3, so East had none left. The Spades might have been divided differently, 4-4. In that case, East would have a Spade left when he won the Ace of Diamonds. But now the opponents could only take a total of three Spade tricks and you would still make your contract.

What if West had the Ace of Diamonds? There is a quotation that is relevant when we are facing such a situation: "Have the courage to change the things you can; the patience to accept the things you cannot change; and the wisdom to know the difference." If West had the Ace of Diamonds and enough Spades to defeat your contract, there was nothing you could do about it. Congratulate yourself for making your best effort.

The hold-up play refers to holding up a sure winner, but it doesn't have to be an Ace. It could be a King. Look at this suit:

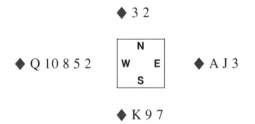

West leads the Five of Diamonds against your No Trump contract. East wins the trick with the Ace and leads the Jack of Diamonds. With the Ace gone, your King has been promoted to a winner. If you play your King now, you will win the trick but, when the opponents get in, either East or West, they will be able to take their Diamond winners because East still has a link card. By holding up on your King, you remove the link card from East with the hope of stranding winners in West's hand.

Here is an example of how the King can be held up to control the opponents' long suit.

Contract: Three No Trump

West leads ♠7

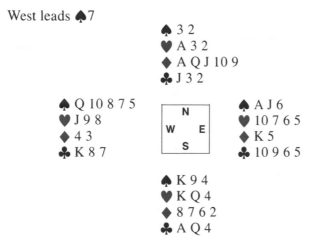

```
                    ♠ 3 2
                    ♥ A 3 2
                    ♦ A Q J 10 9
                    ♣ J 3 2
♠ Q 10 8 7 5                        ♠ A J 6
♥ J 9 8          N                  ♥ 10 7 6 5
♦ 4 3        W       E              ♦ K 5
♣ K 8 7          S                  ♣ 10 9 6 5
                    ♠ K 9 4
                    ♥ K Q 4
                    ♦ 8 7 6 2
                    ♣ A Q 4
```

East wins the opening lead with the Ace of Spades and leads back the Jack of Spades. You need to take nine tricks to reach your goal. You have one sure Spade trick after East takes the Ace, three sure Heart tricks, one Diamond and one Club, for a total of six tricks. You need to develop three more.

This should be easy to do in the Diamond suit, because you are missing only the King. You can hope that West has the King and try a finesse, leading toward dummy and playing the Queen if West plays a small card. If East doesn't have the King, your finesse will work. Even if East does have the King, you will still have promoted enough Diamond winners to make your contract.

However, in putting it all together, you have to watch the opponents. Once you take a trick with your King of Spades, the opponents are ready to take their Spade winners as soon as they find an opportunity. Suppose you win the second trick with your King. On this hand, when you try the Diamond finesse, it loses to East's King. East still has the Six of Spades left as a link card to West. The defense will be able to take four Spades plus the King of Diamonds, and defeat the contract.

You have to use the hold-up play to come out on top in this hand. After East wins the Ace and leads the Jack of Spades, you must hold up your King. Let the Jack win the trick and wait until East leads his last Spade, the Six. What a difference! Now, when you go to establish the Diamonds and East wins a trick with the King, he has no link card to get back to West's winners in Spades. West's Spades are stranded. East will have to lead back a Heart, Club or Diamond, which you can win and then take enough tricks to make your contract.

The hold-up play worked with the King because once the Ace was played, the King became a sure winner. Consider this example:

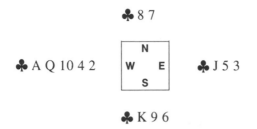

You are playing in a No Trump contract and West leads the Four of Clubs. You play low from dummy, East plays the Jack and it is your turn to play. The Ace has not yet been played, and so the King is a sure trick only if you take it right now.

If you hold up the King, you may never take a trick in the Club suit. East will lead another Club and your King will be trapped by West's Ace and Queen. The defense will take the first five Club tricks and this could be enough to set your contract. Even though you are nervous about what the opponents will do if they regain the lead, you have no choice and cannot afford to hold up. Let's look at a complete hand:

Contract: Three No Trump

West leads ♠6

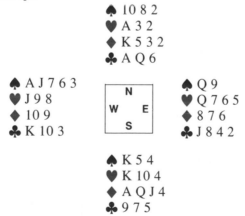

West leads the Six of Spades, you play a small Spade from dummy and East plays the Queen. Should you hold up your King? Always go through the planning steps before making a decision. You need to take nine tricks to reach your goal. You have a Spade winner if you take your King now.

You also have two Heart winners, four Diamonds and one Club . . . a total of eight tricks. You need one more. Where can it come from? With the Queen of Clubs in dummy, you can try a finesse by leading toward the card with which you hope to take a trick, the Queen. If West has the King, you will win two Club tricks; if East has the King, you will win only one.

In putting it all together, will it help to hold up your King? On this hand it will do no good. First, if you don't take your King, you may not get a trick with it. On this hand, the defense will lead a Spade back and take the first five tricks, defeating your contract before you even have a chance. Even if the opponents' Spades were divided 4-4, you would now lose your eighth trick and need two more to make your contract. Secondly, your only hope is that West has the King of Clubs. If East has it, you are never going to get a ninth trick, so the hold-up play will not help.

Your analysis tells you that this is not the time for a hold-up play. The King isn't a sure winner unless you take it now and holding up will do no good if East has the King of Clubs. So win the first trick and stake everything on the Club finesse and you will make your contract!

The Dangerous Opponent

If you have to let the opponents win a trick, it is sometimes more dangerous to let one of the opponents win it rather than the other. For example, suppose you are in a contract of Three No Trump and the player on your left has led a Spade. You have two small Spades in the dummy, and the Ace and two small Spades in your hand. You use the hold-up play and win the third Spade trick. Who is most likely to be your dangerous opponent? The player on your left, who probably started with the long Spade suit. Since the suit has been played three times, he likely has two Spade winners ready when he regains the lead. The player on your right is safer, having no link cards left to partner's Spades.

Suppose you have a suit with the King and two small cards in dummy and some small cards in your hand. You would like to win a trick with your King. If the opponent on your left leads the suit, the King could be trapped should the opponent on your right have the Ace. If your right-hand opponent leads the suit, you play last and can always take a trick with the King. In this situation, the opponent on your left is more dangerous.

It is better to have one **dangerous opponent** and one **safe opponent** than it is to have two dangerous opponents. You have seen how the hold-up play makes one of your opponents safe because he has no link cards to get back to the long suit in his partner's hand. If declarer has to lose a trick, his plan should be to have the trick won by the safe opponent. You might keep in mind the maxim **avoid the dangerous opponent**.

Contract: Three No Trump

West leads ◆K

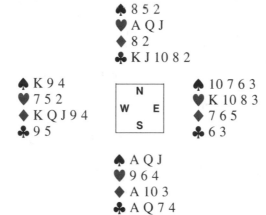

```
                     ♠ 8 5 2
                     ♥ A Q J
                     ◆ 8 2
                     ♣ K J 10 8 2

   ♠ K 9 4                          ♠ 10 7 6 3
   ♥ 7 5 2          N               ♥ K 10 8 3
   ◆ K Q J 9 4   W     E            ◆ 7 6 5
   ♣ 9 5            S               ♣ 6 3

                     ♠ A Q J
                     ♥ 9 6 4
                     ◆ A 10 3
                     ♣ A Q 7 4
```

You need nine tricks. You have one sure Spade trick, one Heart, one Diamond and five Clubs, for a total of eight winners. You need one more. There are two suits that can easily provide the extra trick . . . the Hearts or the Spades. In either suit, you can take a finesse against the King by leading toward the Ace-Queen. Even if the finesse loses, you will still have established the Jack as your ninth trick. Which suit should you play?

To win this hand you must watch the opponents. West has led a Diamond. Once your Ace is dislodged, the opponents will have established their Diamonds as winning tricks. If, as with this hand, the Diamonds are divided 5-3, the opponents will be poised to take four tricks and defeat your contract if you let them win another trick.

To prevent the opponents from being able to take all their tricks, you can start by using the hold-up play. Don't win the first or second trick, but wait until the third trick to take your Diamond Ace. If the suit is divided 5-3, East will not have any Diamonds left. You have created one safe opponent, East, and one dangerous opponent, West.

Now it is easy to see that you should develop your extra trick in Hearts rather than Spades so that you can avoid the dangerous opponent. You can lead a small Heart from your hand to dummy's Queen. If West has the King of Hearts, your Queen will win the trick and you will have enough tricks to make your contract. You could even use an entry back to your hand and repeat the finesse for an **overtrick**. If, as in the actual hand, your finesse loses to East, you are still all right. East is the safe opponent; he has no more Diamonds left. You will be able to win whatever suit East leads back and your Jack of Hearts will have been established as your ninth trick.

Look at the difference if you try to set up your extra trick in Spades. If West has the King, your finesse will lose and you will have let the dangerous opponent have the lead. West will be able to take his remaining two Diamond tricks and defeat your contract.

Keeping an eye on your opponents, as in the above example, can often help you when putting together your plan. Here is an example of a dangerous opponent in a suit contract:

Contract: Four Spades

West leads ♥J

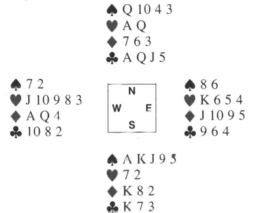

     ♠ Q 10 4 3
     ♥ A Q
     ♦ 7 6 3
     ♣ A Q J 5

♠ 7 2   ♠ 8 6
♥ J 10 9 8 3   ♥ K 6 5 4
♦ A Q 4   ♦ J 10 9 5
♣ 10 8 2   ♣ 9 6 4

     ♠ A K J 9 5
     ♥ 7 2
     ♦ K 8 2
     ♣ K 7 3

You can afford three losers. You have no Spade losers, one potential Heart loser, three potential Diamond losers and no Club losers, for a total of four possible losers. How can you eliminate one of your losers? There are three possibilities. First, you could try the Heart finesse by playing the Queen from dummy. If West has the King, the finesse will work and you will not have a Heart loser. Second, you could plan to lead toward your King of Diamonds, hoping that East has the Ace. If he does, you will only lose two Diamond tricks. Finally, you have an extra winner in the Club suit and you could plan to discard one of your losers on it. Putting it all together, what should you do?

Taking the Heart finesse is fraught with danger. If it loses to East's King, you have just let the dangerous opponent on lead. Why is East dangerous? If East wins a trick, he may lead a Diamond. If West has the Ace of Diamonds, your King will be trapped and you will lose three Diamond tricks. Take a look at the actual hand and see what happens if you play the Queen of Hearts at trick one and East wins the King and leads the Jack of Diamonds. You will lose four tricks and be defeated in your contract.

The safe way to make your contract is to win the first trick with the Ace of Hearts and plan to discard one of your losers on the extra Club in dummy. You will have to play the trump suit first (more about that in Chapter Seven). Watching your opponents, especially the dangerous one, pays dividends on hands of this nature.

You have seen a couple of methods you can use to make it difficult for your opponents to take their winners. Now, let's see what the opponents might be doing to prevent you from taking your winners.

The Opponents Make Things Difficult

You have seen the importance of entries when you are trying to build extra tricks. Timing is important. If entries are used too soon, suits may be stranded. One of the opponents' aims is to make you play your entries before you are ready. Sometimes you can counter what they are trying to do; at other times you cannot. There is no disgrace in not making a contract—it happens frequently in the best of bridge circles. If the opponents play their cards skillfully and prevent you from making your contract, it is best to appreciate the beauty in the way they worked with each other. You can't do anything to change some things and feeling otherwise wastes too much energy.

Declarer is not the only player who can make use of the hold-up play in a No Trump contract. If the defenders have only one sure trick in a suit, they can take it at any time they choose. They may try to strand your winners. Consider this suit:

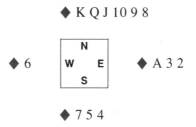

◆ K Q J 10 9 8

◆ 6   ◆ A 3 2

◆ 7 5 4

You are playing in a No Trump contract. The only high cards you have in dummy are in the Diamond suit. By driving out the opponents' Ace, you hope to establish five winners in the suit. If East wins the first or second trick when you lead this suit, you will still have a link card left in your hand as an entry to dummy's remaining winners.

But look what happens if East holds up his Ace until the third time the suit is played. You will win the first two tricks in Diamonds, but will have no link card left to get over to your remaining winners. Unless you have an entry in another suit, your three Diamond winners are stranded.

There is nothing you can do to change this result if you have no entry to the dummy. The defenders' hold-up play has held you to only two tricks. Fortunately, you can usually counter their hold-up play if you plan the hand carefully.

Contract: One No Trump

West leads ♠Q

```
                    ♠ A 2
                    ♥ J 3 2
                    ♦ Q J 10 7 3
                    ♣ 4 3 2

  ♠ Q J 10 7 5      ┌─────────┐      ♠ 9 8 4
  ♥ K 10 9 8        │    N    │      ♥ Q 5 4
  ♦ 8 4             │ W     E │      ♦ A 9 5
  ♣ Q 10            │    S    │      ♣ K J 9 8
                    └─────────┘

                    ♠ K 6 3
                    ♥ A 7 6
                    ♦ K 6 2
                    ♣ A 7 6 5
```

To make your One No Trump contract you need seven tricks. You have two tricks in Spades, one Heart and one Club, for a total of four tricks. You need three more. The Diamond suit offers a chance to promote four winners by driving out the Ace.

The opponents are going to try to eliminate your entries so that you have difficulty promoting your Diamond winners. If you are careful, though, their attempts will not work. If you are careless, however, you may wonder where your tricks went when the hand is over.

The opening lead is the Queen of Spades. Let's see what happens if you play the hand without paying attention to the fourth step of the plan—how do I put it all together? Suppose you take the first trick in the dummy with the Ace of Spades. Next you play the Diamonds because you want to get extra tricks from this suit. You play a Diamond to your King (high card from the short hand) and lead a Diamond back to dummy's Queen. You continue by playing the Jack, then East, who has been holding up, finally takes the Ace. East leads another Spade, returning his partner's suit. You win the trick with the King in your hand. You have taken the Ace and the King of Spades and the King and the Queen of Diamonds, a total of four tricks. You have the Ace of Clubs and the Ace of Hearts, which brings your total to six tricks. There are two good Diamonds in dummy but they are stranded. You will end up one trick short of making your contract.

Now, let's see what happens if you take the time to make a complete plan. After the opening lead of the Queen of Spades, pause for a moment before deciding whether to win the trick with dummy's Ace or your King. You plan to establish the Diamond suit and, if the opponents hold up their Ace, you will need an entry to the dummy to reach your winners. This reasoning makes it clear that you should win the first trick with the King of Spades in your hand. Now you can go to work on the Diamonds. Even if the opponents hold up their Ace, you will have the entry you need to get to dummy's winners. You will end up making an overtrick with two Spade tricks, one Heart trick, four Diamond tricks and one Club trick ... quite a difference!

Sometimes, no matter how you try, you cannot make your contract because the opponents eliminate one of your entries too soon. Have the patience to accept the things you cannot change.

Contract: Three No Trump

West leads ♠J

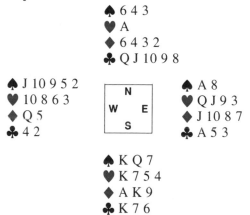

The Jack of Spades is led and East wins the trick with the Ace. At this point, declarer appears to be in a good position. You have two sure Spade tricks now that the Ace is gone, two Heart tricks and two Diamond tricks. In addition, you can drive out the opponents' Ace of Clubs and promote four winners in the Club suit.

Unfortunately, your opponent, East, can see that there is a long Club suit in dummy that you will try to establish. Even if East holds up his Ace of Clubs until you have no link cards left in that suit, he can see that the Ace of Hearts is an entry to the dummy. What can he do to spoil your plans? Instead of leading back a Spade, he can lead a Heart and make you play dummy's Ace before you are ready. Now, when he holds up his Ace of Clubs until the third round of the suit, you have no entry to dummy.

Struggle as you might, you will only be able to make eight tricks: two Spades, two Hearts, two Diamonds and only two Clubs. With this hand there was nothing you could have done to make your contract. The opponents defended well. East eliminated your entry to the dummy before you had a chance to set up your suit. Then he held up on the Club suit to get rid of your link cards before you were ready to take your winners.

Since this is a book for the declarer, let's leave this section on a positive note. Even though the opponents are trying to defeat your contract, there is often a counter-measure you can take . . . if you keep an eye on your opponents.

Contract: One No Trump

West leads ♥Q

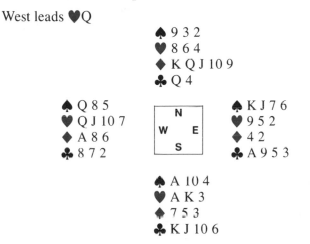

```
                    ♠ 9 3 2
                    ♥ 8 6 4
                    ♦ K Q J 10 9
                    ♣ Q 4
  ♠ Q 8 5                          ♠ K J 7 6
  ♥ Q J 10 7       ┌─────────┐     ♥ 9 5 2
  ♦ A 8 6          │    N    │     ♦ 4 2
  ♣ 8 7 2          │ W     E │     ♣ A 9 5 3
                   │    S    │
                   └─────────┘
                    ♠ A 10 4
                    ♥ A K 3
                    ♦ 7 5 3
                    ♣ K J 10 6
```

You need seven tricks, but you start out with only three winners, the Ace of Spades and the Ace and the King of Hearts. You can establish four extra winners in Diamonds by driving out the Ace, or you can promote three extra tricks in Clubs. Since you need four tricks, it looks like you should establish the Diamond suit.

Yet what will you do if the opponents hold up their Ace? You will end up with no link cards in your hand and no sure winner in dummy to act as an entry. Can you do anything to prevent this result? Yes, if you take it into account in your plan.

You do not need to take all four of the extra tricks you need from the Diamond suit. You could obtain some of them from the Club suit. You should plan to start off by trying to establish the Diamond suit. You win the first Heart trick and lead a small Diamond to dummy's King. If the opponents do not play the Ace, you can lead the suit again. The opponents will probably not play their Ace the second time either. They don't want you to have a link card left. Now there is no point in playing the Diamond suit again. The opponents have successfully foiled your attempt to establish the suit.

However, this doesn't stop you from making the contract. Since you have already got two Diamond tricks, you can switch your attention to the Club suit. You can lead the Queen, high card from the short side, and continue leading the suit until the opponents play their Ace. Thus, you will promote three tricks in the Club suit. When these tricks are added to your other tricks, the sum is more than enough to make your contract.

Summary

When you come to the final step of your plan—how do I put it all together?—you have several aspects of play to consider. In the last chapter you saw that you must watch your entries while carrying out your plans. In this chapter you saw that you must also consider what your opponents are up to.

KEY MAXIM

Watch Your Opponents

There are two ways you can make it more difficult for the opponents to take their tricks: 1) **hold up your ace, 2) avoid the dangerous opponent.**

The first guideline reminds you that you don't have to take your sure winner right away in a suit that the opponents have led. Sometimes it is better to wait until one of your opponents has no link cards left in the suit. The second guideline reminds you to avoid losing a trick to the opponent that is in a position to do harm to your contract. If you must lose a trick, try to lose it to the opponent who can do you no harm.

When the opponents make it difficult for you to take your tricks by using the hold-up play and trying to make you play your sure tricks before you are ready, try to counter their attempt by using your entries wisely. Play the high card from the short side when developing your tricks and keep the entries with the long suit you are establishing as long as possible. If you can't do anything to stop the opponents from defeating your contract, accept it graciously.

Exercises

1) You are in a contract of Three No Trump. Keeping an eye on the opponents, make your plan and decide how to put it all together to make your contract.

♠ A 5 3
♥ A 9 7 6
♦ Q 10 2
♣ K 5 3

West leads ♠7

```
    N
W       E
    S
```

♠ 6 4
♥ K 5 4
♦ K J 8 7 6
♣ A Q 7

Solution

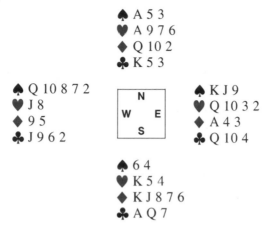

♠ A 5 3
♥ A 9 7 6
♦ Q 10 2
♣ K 5 3

♠ Q 10 8 7 2
♥ J 8
♦ 9 5
♣ J 9 6 2

♠ K J 9
♥ Q 10 3 2
♦ A 4 3
♣ Q 10 4

♠ 6 4
♥ K 5 4
♦ K J 8 7 6
♣ A Q 7

Step One: *How many winners do I need?*

You need nine tricks.

Step Two: *How many winners do I have?*

Spades: 1
Hearts: 2
Diamonds: 0
Clubs: 3
Total: 6

Step Three: *How can I develop extra winners?*

You can drive out the Ace of Diamonds and promote four extra tricks in thc Diamond suit.

Step Four: *How do I put it all together?*

Watch the opponents . . . what could they do to interfere with what looks like a straightforward contract? Once you take the Ace of Spades, thc opponents will be in a position to take their remaining Spade winners. You have only five and they have eight—an even number. They can be expected to break 5-3. In addition, they can take the Ace of Diamonds.

To counter their moves, use thc hold-up play. Take the Spade trick on the third round. Then go after the Diamonds, playing the high card, the Queen, from the short side. When East takes the Ace, hc has no Spades to play and West's Spade winners are stranded. Whatever East returns, you win and make your contract.

2) This time you are in One No Trump. How do you plan to make your contract?

♠ A Q 8 7 6
♥ A 6 2
♦ J 2
♣ Q 5 3

West leads ♥ 10

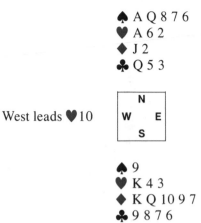

♠ 9
♥ K 4 3
♦ K Q 10 9 7
♣ 9 8 7 6

Solution

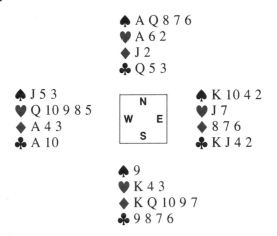

♠ A Q 8 7 6
♥ A 6 2
♦ J 2
♣ Q 5 3

♠ J 5 3
♥ Q 10 9 8 5
♦ A 4 3
♣ A 10

♠ K 10 4 2
♥ J 7
♦ 8 7 6
♣ K J 4 2

♠ 9
♥ K 4 3
♦ K Q 10 9 7
♣ 9 8 7 6

Step One: *How many winners do I need?*

You need to take seven tricks.

Step Two: *How many winners do I have?*

Spades:	1
Hearts:	2
Diamonds:	0
Clubs:	0
Total:	3

Step Three: *How can I develop extra winners?*

The Four extra winners can be promoted in the Diamond suit.

Step Four: *How do I put it all together?*

Watch out for the opponents. They may make it difficult for you by not winning the first trick with their Ace of Diamonds. You will have no link cards left in the Diamond suit. Keep the King of Hearts as an entry.

Win the first trick with your Ace of Hearts. Play the high card from the short side, the Jack of Diamonds. Continue leading Diamonds until the opponents take their Ace. The King of Hearts is an entry to your Diamond winners no matter what the opponents do.

Where you take the first trick will determine the success or failure of your contract.

3) You are in a contract of Three Clubs. Keeping an eye on the damage
that the opponents might do, how do you plan to make the contract?

♠ A Q 8 7
♥ 6 3
♦ 10 8 7 6 5
♣ 4 2

West leads ♥J

```
    N
W       E
    S
```

♠ 4 3
♥ A K 2
♦ Q 3
♣ K Q J 10 8 7

Solution

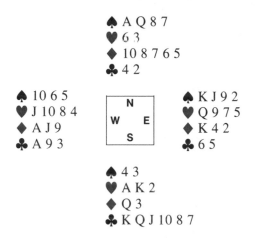

♠ A Q 8 7
♥ 6 3
♦ 10 8 7 6 5
♣ 4 2

♠ 10 6 5
♥ J 10 8 4
♦ A J 9
♣ A 9 3

♠ K J 9 2
♥ Q 9 7 5
♦ K 4 2
♣ 6 5

♠ 4 3
♥ A K 2
♦ Q 3
♣ K Q J 10 8 7

Step One: *How many losers can I afford?*

You can afford four losers.

Step Two: *How many losers do I have?*

Spades:	1
Hearts:	1
Diamonds:	2
Clubs:	1
Total:	5

Step Three: *How can I eliminate losers?*

In Spades you could try the finesse; if it works you would have no losers. In Hearts, you could plan to ruff your Heart loser in dummy. There is no chance of escaping the other losers.

Step Four: *How do I put it all together?*

Are entries a problem? No. There are two entries to your hand, enough to either try the finesse or be in the right place to ruff the third Heart trick. Does it matter which you do first? Suppose you decide to start with the Spade finesse, to see if it works. If it doesn't, you plan to ruff the third Heart in the dummy. Sounds like a reasonable plan . . . but watch the opponents.

If the Spade finesse fails, as it does on the above hand, East may turn out to be a dangerous opponent and lead a trump. West can win the trick and play another trump. Now you have no trumps left in the dummy and will lose a Spade, a Heart, two Clubs and a Diamond.

You should avoid giving a dangerous opponent the opportunity to lead. First play the Ace, the King and another Heart, ruffing it in the dummy. Now you have eliminated one of your losers and cannot be thwarted by the opponents in making your contract. Later, you can try the Spade finesse for an overtrick.

5

Take Your Tricks and Run

One of the most delightful maxims in bridge is **take your tricks and run**. You have the tricks you need . . . all you have to do is take them. Have you ever played with friends whom you feel are much better players than you and secretly, or not so secretly, hoped that you were the dummy rather than the declarer whenever your side played the contract? When you apply this advice—take your tricks and run—you no longer have to hope that you don't get any high cards. You can be confident that you can play such hands as well as the best of players.

Take your tricks and run applies in both No Trump and suit contracts. The basic idea is that when you have the number of winners you need in a No Trump contract or the number of losers you can afford in a suit contract, you should go ahead and take your tricks. Aesop has a fable that describes a dog with a good-sized bone walking across a bridge over a clear pond. He catches his reflection and drops the bone in an effort to get what appears to be an even bigger prize. Your first priority is to make your contract. Don't put it in jeopardy in an effort to make an even bigger score.

There is a variation. When you don't have enough tricks to reach your goal, consider whether your losers are quick or slow. A **quick loser** is one that the opponents will take as soon as you give them the lead. A **slow loser** is one that the opponents could get eventually but, before they do,

84

they have to give the lead back to you. If your losers are quick, you will have to try to take your tricks and run, devising a plan for the play that, although it doesn't guarantee the contract, doesn't let you **give up the lead**.

When You Have Enough Tricks

When you know that you have enough tricks to reach your goal, what could possibly go wrong? At times, your sure tricks will be divided unevenly between the two hands, and when this happens, you must pay special attention to your entries: play the high card from the short side; keep your high cards with the long suit until you are ready to take your tricks. Another thing that could go wrong: you might forget that the opponents are ready to take their tricks as soon as you give them the lead. Remember that your first priority is to make your contract. Let's start off with a typical example:

Contract: One No Trump

West leads ♠Q

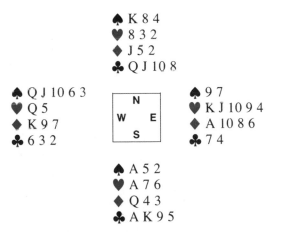

```
                    ♠ K 8 4
                    ♥ 8 3 2
                    ♦ J 5 2
                    ♣ Q J 10 8

    ♠ Q J 10 6 3         N          ♠ 9 7
    ♥ Q 5                           ♥ K J 10 9 4
    ♦ K 9 7         W       E       ♦ A 10 8 6
    ♣ 6 3 2             S           ♣ 7 4

                    ♠ A 5 2
                    ♥ A 7 6
                    ♦ Q 4 3
                    ♣ A K 9 5
```

Your goal is to take seven tricks. Count the winners: Spades, 2; Hearts, 1; Diamonds, 0; Clubs, 4. You have no extra tricks to develop. Take your tricks and run! How are you going to do it? Are there any entry problems? You have enough link cards to take your Spades, Hearts and Clubs. Your friends may even compliment you by saying that one-level contracts are often the toughest to make!

Let's look at another example that is straightforward . . . if you resist temptation.

Contract: Four Spades

West leads ♥J

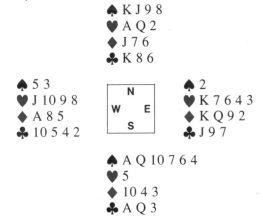

The Jack of Hearts has been led. What do you play from the dummy? As you know from Chapter One, it is possible to develop an extra winner by taking a finesse. You could play the Queen and, if West has the King, you will get two Heart tricks instead of one. If East has the King, you will only get one trick. Do you take the finesse? Before deciding what to do, you need to make your plan for the whole hand.

To achieve your objective, you can afford only three losers. You have no Spade losers, no Heart losers, three Diamond losers and no Club losers, for a total of three. You know you can reach your goal. On the other hand, you can't afford to create an extra loser. By giving in to the temptation of the Heart finesse and playing the Queen, you may . . . and, in playing the actual hand, will . . . give yourself a Heart loser you hadn't counted on. The opponents should have little difficulty taking their three Diamond tricks once East gets the lead with the King of Hearts.

Since there are no extra losers to eliminate, take your tricks and run. Don't feel you have to take a finesse just because it is there. Win the first trick with the Ace of Hearts, draw trump, take your sure Club tricks and make the contract.

Entries are always a consideration—even when you have the number of tricks you need to make your contract.

Contract: One No Trump

West leads ♠J

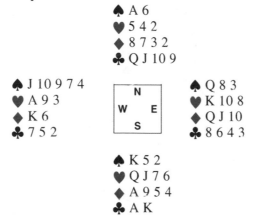

```
                    ♠ A 6
                    ♥ 5 4 2
                    ♦ 8 7 3 2
                    ♣ Q J 10 9

♠ J 10 9 7 4            N            ♠ Q 8 3
♥ A 9 3          W         E         ♥ K 10 8
♦ K 6                  S             ♦ Q J 10
♣ 7 5 2                              ♣ 8 6 4 3

                    ♠ K 5 2
                    ♥ Q J 7 6
                    ♦ A 9 5 4
                    ♣ A K
```

You are in One No Trump and your goal is to take seven tricks. There are enough winners: Spades, 2; Hearts, 0; Diamonds, 1; Clubs, 4. It looks like a simple case of take your tricks and run. However, in the fourth step of your plan—How do I put it all together?—don't forget the other guidelines we have already discussed.

There are four sure tricks in Clubs, but the suit is unevenly divided so you must plan to play the high card (in this case, the high cards) from the short side first. Having done this, you will still be in your hand and will need an entry to get to the dummy to enjoy the last two Club winners. That means you must watch your entries. Win the opening lead with the King of Spades in your hand, keeping the Ace of Spades in the dummy until you have played the Ace and the King of Clubs. That way you avoid stranding the Club winners. You can play a small Spade to dummy's Ace and take the remaining two Club winners. Finally, the Ace of Diamonds will be your seventh trick.

There are not that many hands that you get to play in a Grand Slam, but if you do, you want to be sure to make it . . . it's always a good topic of conversation until the next game. So let's look at an example.

Contract: Seven No Trump

West leads ♣10

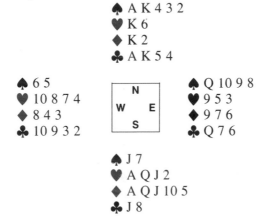

♠ A K 4 3 2
♥ K 6
♦ K 2
♣ A K 5 4

♠ 6 5
♥ 10 8 7 4
♦ 8 4 3
♣ 10 9 3 2

♠ Q 10 9 8
♥ 9 5 3
♦ 9 7 6
♣ Q 7 6

♠ J 7
♥ A Q J 2
♦ A Q J 10 5
♣ J 8

Your goal is to take thirteen tricks . . . let's hope you are not superstitious. Will your winners add up to thirteen? Spades, 2; Hearts, 4; Diamonds, 5; Clubs, 2. You have enough tricks. The suits are unevenly distributed, which means you must be careful about the order in which the tricks are taken so you don't end up in the wrong hand at the wrong time. Make use of the maxim play the high card from the short side.

Win the opening Club lead with dummy's Ace of Clubs. Since you have all of the tricks, look at the hand one suit at a time and take your winners. You are in the dummy. Play the Ace and the King of Spades. Now look at the Hearts. The first trick has to be won with the King, high card from the short side. Next play the Six of Hearts over to the Ace, Queen, Jack in your hand, throwing low Spades and Clubs from the dummy. Be careful not to throw away a small Diamond from dummy because that will be your link card back to your hand. You are now in your hand. Play your Five of Diamonds over to the King, the high card from the short side. Play the Two of Diamonds back to the winners in your hand. As you play your winning Diamonds, discard the remaining small cards from the dummy, keeping only the King of Clubs. You have your thirteen tricks after you lead to dummy's remaining card, the King of Clubs.

Now let's return our attention to hands in which you don't have enough tricks to reach your goal.

When You Don't Have Enough Tricks

When you lack the number of tricks necessary to reach your goal, your first step is to consider the nature of the tricks you might have to lose: are they quick or slow losers? If they are quick, then you can't let the opponents have the lead. You must devise a plan where you take your tricks and run, although you are not sure if you will reach the finish line. Let's see how it works.

Contract: Three No Trump

West leads ♥5

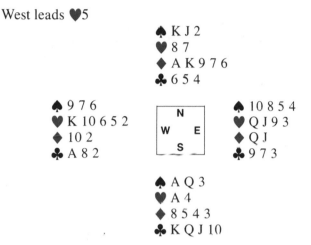

You need nine tricks. You have three sure tricks in Spades, one in Hearts, two in Diamonds and none in Clubs, for a total of six tricks. You need to develop three more tricks to make the contract. One source of tricks is the Club suit. You can establish the extra tricks you need through promotion after driving out the opponents' Ace.

Another possible source of tricks is the Diamond suit. You have nine Diamonds, so the opponents only have four. If they are divided 2-2, you will be able to establish three extra tricks through length. You can play your Ace and King and the opponents will have no cards left in the suit. Of course, as you saw in Chapter One, it is more likely that the opponents' Diamonds will break 3-1. In that case, you will win only two extra tricks because you will have to give up a trick to the opponents. The Diamonds might even break 4-0.

How do you put it all together? On the surface, it looks as though you should play the Clubs and establish three extra winners no matter how the suit is divided. But watch the opponents! West has led a Heart and, even if you hold up and don't take the first trick, you will be forced to win the second trick. Both opponents will still have some Hearts left; you cannot get rid of one opponent's link cards. You have only four Hearts and the opponents have nine. The best distribution you could hope for is 5-4. After your Ace is gone, if you let the opponents win another trick, they will also get at least four Heart tricks and defeat your contract. You would have five quick losers.

This warns you that you cannot try to get your extra tricks by driving out the Ace of Clubs. It will lead to certain defeat. Instead, you must try to take your tricks and run, even though there is no certainty that it will work. Your only hope is to play the Ace and the King of Diamonds and hope that the suit divides 2-2.

Here is another example in which you have too many quick losers:

Contract: Three No Trump

West leads ♠7

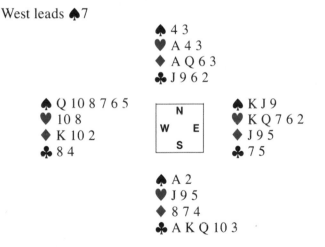

```
                    ♠ 4 3
                    ♥ A 4 3
                    ♦ A Q 6 3
                    ♣ J 9 6 2

♠ Q 10 8 7 6 5          N          ♠ K J 9
♥ 10 8                            ♥ K Q 7 6 2
♦ K 10 2          W       E        ♦ J 9 5
♣ 8 4                  S           ♣ 7 5

                    ♠ A 2
                    ♥ J 9 5
                    ♦ 8 7 4
                    ♣ A K Q 10 3
```

You need nine tricks to make your contract. You have one Spade, one Heart, one Diamond and five Clubs, for a total of eight tricks. You need one more and the only source is the Diamond suit. You can take a finesse and hope that West has the King. There is no chance for an extra trick in the other suits.

The opponents have led a Spade and, once your Ace is gone, you will have too many quick losers if you let them get the lead too soon. This is another hand in which you should try to take your tricks and run. You can take all of your sure tricks in Spades, Hearts and Clubs first, but the entire success or failure of your contract depends on whether the Diamond finesse is successful.

If you are going to take your other sure tricks first, be sure to watch your entries and end up in your hand so that you can lead a small Diamond toward the Ace and Queen in dummy. For example, win the Ace of Spades, play a Heart to the Ace, lead the Jack of Clubs (high card from the short side) and then a small Club to your hand. After taking all your Club winners, play a small Diamond and, when West plays a small Diamond, play your Queen and keep your fingers crossed!

In this final example, you are playing in a trump contract and have too many quick losers if the opponents get the lead. Once again, you must devise a plan that will allow you to take your tricks and run.

Contract: Four Hearts

West leads ♣K

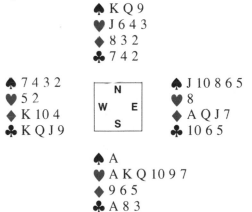

```
                    ♠ K Q 9
                    ♥ J 6 4 3
                    ♦ 8 3 2
                    ♣ 7 4 2
    ♠ 7 4 3 2                      ♠ J 10 8 6 5
    ♥ 5 2          N              ♥ 8
    ♦ K 10 4    W     E           ♦ A Q J 7
    ♣ K Q J 9      S              ♣ 10 6 5
                    ♠ A
                    ♥ A K Q 10 9 7
                    ♦ 9 6 5
                    ♣ A 8 3
```

You can afford three losers. You have no Spade losers, no Heart losers, three Diamond losers and two Club losers. You need to eliminate two of your losers. Can you afford to give up the lead to the opponents? No, your losers are all quick losers. If you give the opponents a chance, they will take their four tricks. How can you get rid of your losers? You have two extra Spade winners in dummy so you can plan to discard two of your losers.

It is really a straightforward case of take your tricks and run. However, as always, you must be careful with your entries. To discard your losers you must first play your Ace of Spades, high card from the short side. Now you need an entry to the dummy, since you have no link cards in Spades. The only possible entry is the Jack of Hearts. You must play a small Heart to your Jack and then you can play the King and the Queen of Spades and discard two of your losers.

Summary

```
┌─────────────────────────────────────────────┐
│                                             │
│                  KEY MAXIM                  │
│                                             │
│           Take Your Tricks And Run          │
│                                             │
└─────────────────────────────────────────────┘
```

Take your tricks and run is part of keeping your eye on your objective. The key to when to use it comes from making your plan.

If you have enough tricks to reach your goal . . . take your tricks and run. Don't try to take an extra trick when it might jeopardize the contract. Notice if your suits are unevenly divided between the two hands. If they are, watch your entries. Play the high card from the short side when taking tricks in your long suit. Make sure you keep your entries with the long suit until you are ready to take tricks in that suit.

If you don't have enough tricks, consider whether your losers are quick or slow. If they are quick, you can't let the opponents have the lead, so plan to try to take your tricks and run. The key to developing the extra tricks you need is to choose a line of play that prevents the opponents from getting the lead.

Exercises

1) You are in a contract of Three No Trump. Make a plan and decide whether to take your tricks and run.

$$\spadesuit\ A\ K\ 3$$
$$\heartsuit\ K\ 6\ 4\ 3$$
$$\diamondsuit\ A\ 8\ 3\ 2$$
$$\clubsuit\ A\ J$$

West leads ♥5

```
      N
  W       E
      S
```

$$\spadesuit\ 7\ 6\ 2$$
$$\heartsuit\ A\ 8\ 2$$
$$\diamondsuit\ 9\ 6\ 5$$
$$\clubsuit\ K\ Q\ 3\ 2$$

Solution

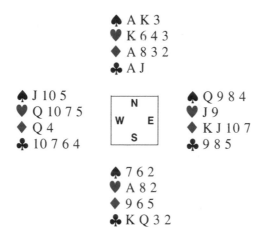

♠ A K 3
♥ K 6 4 3
♦ A 8 3 2
♣ A J

♠ J 10 5
♥ Q 10 7 5
♦ Q 4
♣ 10 7 6 4

♠ Q 9 8 4
♥ J 9
♦ K J 10 7
♣ 9 8 5

♠ 7 6 2
♥ A 8 2
♦ 9 6 5
♣ K Q 3 2

Note: By now you should be familiar with the four planning steps and we won't repeat them in each answer. The solution will still go through the steps, but in paragraph form, as the hand might be discussed in a newspaper bridge column.

You need nine tricks. You have two Spade winners, two Hearts, one Diamond and four Clubs . . . nine tricks. You have what you need so you can take your tricks and run. How do you put it all together? First, consider the entries. The Club suit is unevenly divided and the long suit is in your hand. Make sure you keep an entry with that suit until you need it. Win the opening lead with the King of Hearts in the dummy. Play the high cards from the short side, the Ace and the Jack of Clubs. Next, come over to your hand with the Ace of Hearts and take the last two Clubs, the King and the Queen. You can take the Ace and the King of Spades and the Ace of Diamonds for your nine tricks.

2) You are in Three No Trump. West leads the Heart Four and East plays the Jack. Should you win with your King of Hearts or hold up? How do you plan to make the contract?

♠ 9 8 2
♥ 9
♦ Q 8 5 3
♣ A K 7 5 2

West leads ♥4

```
      N
  W       E
      S
```

♠ A K 4
♥ K 7 6
♦ A K 7 2
♣ 9 6 3

Solution

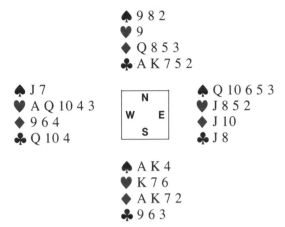

```
            ♠ 9 8 2
            ♥ 9
            ♦ Q 8 5 3
            ♣ A K 7 5 2

♠ J 7                        ♠ Q 10 6 5 3
♥ A Q 10 4 3      N          ♥ J 8 5 2
♦ 9 6 4       W     E        ♦ J 10
♣ Q 10 4          S          ♣ J 8

            ♠ A K 4
            ♥ K 7 6
            ♦ A K 7 2
            ♣ 9 6 3
```

You need nine tricks. You have two Spade winners, one Heart winner if you win the King right away, three Diamond winners and two Club winners. How can you develop the extra winner you need? You have eight Clubs and the opponents have five. If the opponents' Clubs break 3-2, you can give them a Club trick and end up taking two extra tricks. Another possible source is the Diamond suit. Again, you have eight cards and the opponents have five. If the opponents' cards divide 3-2, you will have one extra trick from your remaining Diamonds.

Should you play your King of Hearts or hold up? Since the Ace has not been played, the King is not a sure trick. If you don't take it now, you may never get it. East will win the first trick and lead the suit again. On this hand, West will then take the next four tricks and you will be defeated.

After winning the King, should you try for the extra tricks in Clubs or Diamonds? Playing Clubs will give you two extra tricks if the suit is 3-2, whereas the Diamonds will only give you one. But take a look at your quick losers! To establish the Clubs, you will have to lose a trick to the opponents. Since the opponents started with nine Hearts, you will then have to lose at least four Heart tricks.

Instead you should plan to play the Diamonds and hope that they are divided 3-2. Now you can make your contract without giving up a trick to the opponents.

3) You are in a contract of Four Hearts. Can you take your tricks and run?

♠ A 9 2
♥ 7 5 4 2
♦ 10 8 4
♣ A 8 5

West leads ♣J

```
      N
  W       E
      S
```

♠ K Q
♥ A K Q J 10
♦ J 3 2
♣ K 6 3

Solution

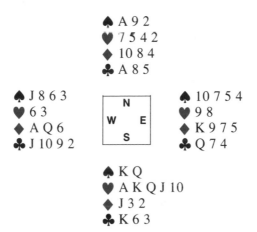

♠ A 9 2
♥ 7 5 4 2
♦ 10 8 4
♣ A 8 5

♠ J 8 6 3
♥ 6 3
♦ A Q 6
♣ J 10 9 2

♠ 10 7 5 4
♥ 9 8
♦ K 9 7 5
♣ Q 7 4

♠ K Q
♥ A K Q J 10
♦ J 3 2
♣ K 6 3

You can afford three losers. You have no losers in Spades and Hearts, three losers in Diamonds and one in Clubs. How can you eliminate one of your losers? Dummy has an extra winner in Spades, so you can plan to discard one of your losers on it.

Can you take your tricks and run? Yes, if you are careful to watch your entries. You will need an entry to dummy to play your extra Spade winner. Since the only entry is the Ace of Clubs, you must win the first trick in your hand with the King. After taking the King and the Queen of Spades, high cards from the short side, you can use the Ace of Clubs to reach dummy and discard one of your losers on the Ace of Spades.

6

Take Your Losses Early

In the previous chapter, we discussed hands in which you either had enough winners or could not afford to lose a trick to the opponents and, therefore, had to take your tricks and run. However, you often don't have enough tricks to make your contract and may have to give up the lead to develop the extra tricks you need. It is a trade-off: you'll give something up with the hope of getting something in return that will help you to reach your objective.

A popular maxim when you have to lose tricks to the opponents is **take your losses early**. Yet this advice contradicts the maxim take your tricks and run. How are you to know which saying best applies to a particular hand? Once again, the key is to make your plan.

In the last chapter, we saw that you take your tricks and run in two cases: if you have enough winners to reach your objective; and if you don't have enough winners, but you have too many quick losers and must devise a way to play the hand without giving up the lead. In this chapter we'll take a look at a situation in which you don't have enough winners (or have too many losers in a suit contract) but can afford to give up the lead to your opponents.

In most hands, it is quite natural for the opponents to win tricks while you are developing the tricks you need. You often have to give up tricks to promote winners, to establish long suits, to take finesses, to discard losers and to trump losers in the dummy. The key is to give them up when it can do you the least harm.

Promoting Winners

Promoting your high cards into winners by driving out the opponents' high cards is a sure method of developing extra winners. Provided you have sufficient high card strength and the required entries, you do not need to rely on any favorable division or position of the opponents' cards. However, to promote high cards, you must give up the lead to the opponents. This is only safe if you do not have too many quick losers. That is, if the opponents are not in a position to take enough tricks to defeat your contract. Let's look at an example:

Contract: Three No Trump

West leads ♥Q

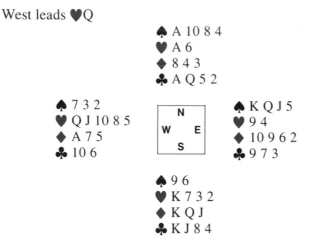

Your objective is to take nine tricks. You have one sure Spade trick, two Heart tricks and four Club tricks. You need to develop two extra tricks. These can be easily developed in the Diamond suit by driving out the opponents' Ace. There will be no entry problem in Diamonds since number of cards in the dummy is equal to the number of cards in your hand.

When you ask yourself "How do I put it all together?", you have to decide whether you should take your sure tricks first and then establish the Diamonds, or whether you should start with the Diamonds. This is when you have to consider taking your losses early.

Suppose you decide to take your sure tricks first. You play the Ace and the King of Hearts, the Ace of Spades and the four Club tricks. Then you lead the King of Diamonds to drive out the opponents' Ace. What will happen? The opponents will be delighted! They will not help you get your Diamonds winners by leading back a Diamond. They will have been busy discarding their little Diamonds and keeping their winners in Hearts and Spades, which you have established for them. You have done your opponents' work for them and created too many quick losers for yourself.

The key is timing . . . start to promote the Diamonds while you still have control of the hand. Having control of the hand means not having too many quick losers when the opponents get the lead. By retaining your winners in other suits, you avoid losing control when the opponents get in.

On this hand, after winning the opening lead with one of your Heart tricks, immediately lead the Diamonds and establish the two extra tricks you need. Once the opponents have played the Ace of Diamonds, there is nothing they can do to stop you from making your contract. Whatever suit they lead, you can win (you have control). Now that you have enough sure tricks, take your tricks and run.

Here is an example in a suit contract:

Contract: Two Diamonds

West leads ♠J

```
                ♠ K 8 3
                ♥ Q J 10
                ♦ A Q 5
                ♣ A 8 4 3

♠ J 10 9 5 2        N        ♠ A Q 6
♥ A 8 4                      ♥ K 6 5 3
♦ 9 6        W        E      ♦ 7 4
♣ K J 7             S        ♣ Q 10 6 5

                ♠ 7 4
                ♥ 9 7 2
                ♦ K J 10 8 3 2
                ♣ 9 2
```

You can afford five losers. You have two Spade losers, two Heart losers (the Ace and the King), no Diamond losers and one Club loser. That looks simple enough. However, the statement that you have only two Heart losers is based on the assumption that you can promote one of your Hearts into a winner by driving out the opponents' Ace and King.

West has led the Jack of Spades. You can try playing dummy's King, but, as it turns out, your King loses to East's Ace. Let's suppose East now takes a trick with the Queen of Spades and leads another Spade. You trump it with one of your Diamonds. Can you take all your sure tricks before going to work on the Hearts?

If you lead all your Diamonds and play the Ace of Clubs, it will be too late to establish the Hearts. When you try to do that, you will find that you have too many quick losers in Spades and Clubs. You must keep your Ace of Clubs to control that suit and you must keep some Diamonds to prevent the opponents from being able to take Spade tricks when they get the lead. You will see in the next chapter that there is good reason to play some of your Diamonds early, to eliminate the opponents' trumps. On this hand, after you draw trump, take your losses early and play Hearts immediately while you still have control. You have to let the opponents in twice to establish your Heart trick, so you must be prepared to handle whatever they lead back each time.

Suit Establishment

Suit establishment through length sometimes requires that you take your losses early.

Contract: One No Trump

West leads ♣Q

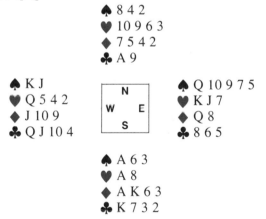

```
                    ♠ 8 4 2
                    ♥ 10 9 6 3
                    ♦ 7 5 4 2
                    ♣ A 9
    ♠ K J                              ♠ Q 10 9 7 5
    ♥ Q 5 4 2         N               ♥ K J 7
    ♦ J 10 9       W     E            ♦ Q 8
    ♣ Q J 10 4        S               ♣ 8 6 5
                    ♠ A 6 3
                    ♥ A 8
                    ♦ A K 6 3
                    ♣ K 7 3 2
```

Your objective is to take seven tricks. You have one sure Spade trick, one Heart, two Diamonds and two Clubs, for a total of six winners. Where can you develop the extra trick? The only suit that has potential is the Diamond suit, your longest combined suit. You have eight Diamonds and the opponents have five. You hope that they are divided 3-2.

You have no entry problems because there are an equal number of cards in the dummy and in your hand. Win the opening lead in either the dummy or your hand and play the Diamond Ace, the Diamond King and a small Diamond. On this hand, the opponents' Diamonds are divided 3-2, as you would normally expect them to be. West will win the third

Diamond trick with the Jack. You will win whatever suit West returns and have developed your seventh trick in the Diamond suit.

By taking your losses early you keep control in the other suits. Try playing the hand by taking your winners before establishing the extra Diamond trick and you will see that you cannot develop enough tricks to make your contract.

What would have happened if the Diamonds were not divided 3-2? You wouldn't have made your contract, but you would have given it your best shot.

Finessing

Here's a hand in which you need to take a finesse to make your contract:

Contract: Three No Trump

West leads: ♦J

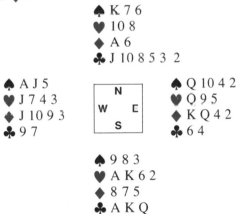

```
                  ♠ K 7 6
                  ♥ 10 8
                  ♦ A 6
                  ♣ J 10 8 5 3 2
    ♠ A J 5                      ♠ Q 10 4 2
    ♥ J 7 4 3          N         ♥ Q 9 5
    ♦ J 10 9 3    W        E     ♦ K Q 4 2
    ♣ 9 7              S         ♣ 6 4
                  ♠ 9 8 3
                  ♥ A K 6 2
                  ♦ 8 7 5
                  ♣ A K Q
```

You need nine tricks. You have two in Hearts, one in Diamonds and six in Clubs. However, there is a problem with entries. The opponents have led Diamonds, and even if you hold up, they will continue until they knock out your Ace, which is your only sure entry to dummy. What can you do?

The King of Spades is a possible entry to dummy, if West has the Ace. You will have to lead toward it and take a finesse. You must put everything together carefully. After winning the Ace of Diamonds, play the Ace, King and Queen of Clubs. Then, lead a small Spade toward dummy. If West plays a small card, you play your King. If West plays the Ace, your King is an entry. Provided East doesn't have the Ace, your King will be the entry you need. You can now take your remaining Club winners and finish off by taking your Heart winners.

Even if West has the Ace, there is still the danger that you may have too many quick losers. East might take the Ace and continue playing Diamonds. In order for you to make your contract, the opponents' Diamonds must be divided 4-4, so that they can't take enough Diamond tricks to defeat you.

As mentioned earlier, you can't afford to give the lead to the opponents if you have too many quick losers. With this hand, you can't be sure that you are going to make your contract. Notice, however, that you cannot afford to play the Ace and the King of Hearts before leading a Spade. If you did that, you would definitely have too many quick losers when you gave up the lead. Once again, you must take your losses early in order to make your contract.

Discarding Losers

When you are in a suit contract and have to discard your losers on extra winners in the dummy, you sometimes have to take your losses early. Look at this example:

Contract: Three Diamonds

West leads ♣A

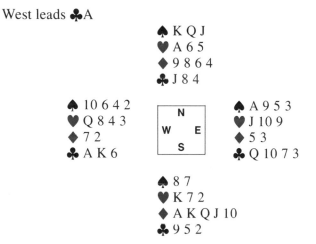

You can afford four losers. You have one Spade loser, one Heart loser, and three Club losers. You need to get rid of a loser. There is no short suit in the dummy to help you trump a loser. You will have to throw a loser on an extra winner. You can promote an extra winner in the Spade suit by driving out the opponents' Ace. Since the suit is unevenly divided between your hand and the dummy, this extra trick will provide a place to discard a loser.

In putting it all together, you must watch your entries. The Ace of Hearts is the only sure entry to the dummy and should be left there, if possible, until the Spades are established. Give up the Spade trick first.

Suppose the opponents take the first three Club tricks and then lead a Heart. Be careful to win it, in your hand, with the King. Once again, you would now play enough Diamonds to get rid of the opponents' trump, but keep the rest to maintain control when you let the opponents in. Then you can lead a small Spade to dummy. If the opponents do not play their Ace on the first trick, you can play the suit again. This time, the opponents must use the Ace or you won't lose any Spade tricks and you will make your contract. Whatever they lead back, you can win, then use your carefully preserved Ace of Hearts as an entry to dummy to play your last Spade and discard your Heart loser. In this example, taking your losses early helps you to keep the entry you need.

When a suit is unevenly divided, you may have to take your losses early by ducking to create an entry within the suit you are establishing. We have seen examples of this approach in Chapter Three. Here, we will combine it with the concept of discarding a loser in a suit contract.

Contract: Four Hearts

West leads ♠K

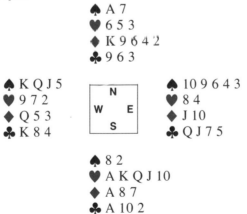

```
              ♠ A 7
              ♥ 6 5 3
              ♦ K 9 6 4 2
              ♣ 9 6 3

♠ K Q J 5                    ♠ 10 9 6 4 3
♥ 9 7 2          N           ♥ 8 4
♦ Q 5 3      W       E       ♦ J 10
♣ K 8 4          S           ♣ Q J 7 5

              ♠ 8 2
              ♥ A K Q J 10
              ♦ A 8 7
              ♣ A 10 2
```

You can afford three losers. You have one Spade loser, one Diamond loser and two Club losers, which is one too many. You have to eliminate a loser. There are no finesses to try, nor are there any losers that can be trumped in dummy. Your only hope is that you can discard one of your losers on an extra winner.

The extra winners in this hand are not immediately evident. You have eight Diamonds in the two hands, and the opponents have five. You could establish one or more extra winners in the Diamond suit.

However, if you are going to establish a suit, you must make sure that you have the entries to enjoy your labors. The opponents have led Spades, so you will have to use up your Ace of Spades before the Diamond suit is established. The only remaining entry to the dummy is the Diamond King.

After you win the Ace of Spades, you will need to play the trump suit (as will be explained in the next chapter) until the opponents have no trump left. With the opponents' trump gone, the hand can be played like a contract in No Trump. Take your losses early. Don't play the Ace and the King of Diamonds first—when you give up a Diamond trick to the opponents, the suit will be established, but it will also be stranded.

Instead, lose the first Diamond trick by playing a small Diamond from both hands (or, you could play the Ace of Diamonds, then lose the second trick in the suit). The opponents can take their Spade trick, but whatever they lead next, you are in control. Win the next trick and play the Ace of Diamonds, followed by your remaining small card to dummy's King. Dummy's remaining two Diamonds are now established as winners when the suit breaks 3-2. Play them and discard both your Club losers.

Trumping Losers

Trumping losers in the dummy is something that often has to be done in suit contracts. On many hands, this involves losing one or more tricks to the opponents. Here is an example:

Contract: Three Spades

West leads: ♣A

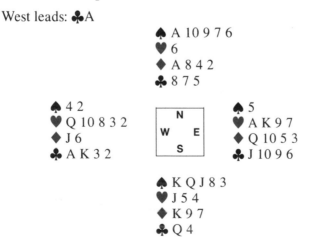

You can afford four losers. You have none in Spades, three in Hearts, one in Diamonds and two in Clubs. You can't do much about the Club losers and there is nowhere to discard the Diamond loser. You might try to establish an extra Diamond winner in dummy if the suit breaks 3-3, and then use the extra winner to discard one of your Heart losers. But that would require a very favorable distribution and would only eliminate one of your losers. It is simpler to plan on trumping both of your Heart losers in dummy.

Suppose the opponents take the first two Club tricks then lead another Club, which you trump. Again, you will see in the next chapter that you should probably get rid of the opponents' trump at this point. However, you cannot keep taking your winners. You have work to do.

You need to trump your Heart losers in the dummy, so you must prepare by giving up a trick to the opponents. Dummy will now be void in Hearts and you have control of whichever suit the opponents lead. You have also retained enough trump in the dummy to trump both of your losers.

This hand illustrates another reason why you do not take all your winners before losing a trick to the opponents. After you trump one of your Heart losers in dummy, you need an entry back to your hand so that you can lead your last Heart and trump it in dummy. You can hold onto the King of Diamonds for this purpose.

Now try this example:

Contract: Two Hearts

West leads ♠3

```
                    ♠ 7 6 5 4
                    ♥ K Q 7
                    ♦ 7 4
                    ♣ Q 8 3 2
   ♠ K J 8 3          ┌─────────┐      ♠ Q 9
   ♥ 6 4              │    N    │      ♥ 5 3 2
   ♦ A J 6 3          │ W     E │      ♦ K Q 9 2
   ♣ J 9 7            │    S    │      ♣ K 10 6 5
                      └─────────┘
                    ♠ A 10 2
                    ♥ A J 10 9 8
                    ♦ 10 8 5
                    ♣ A 4
```

You can afford five losers. You have two Spade losers, three Diamond losers and one Club loser. You notice that dummy only has two Diamonds, whereas you have three. If you can get rid of the two Diamonds in dummy, you can trump your remaining Diamond loser with one of dummy's trumps.

Start taking your losses very early with this hand. After winning East's Queen of Spades with your Ace, you cannot afford to play even one of your Heart tricks before leading Diamonds. Let's see what happens if you do.

Suppose you play a Heart to dummy's King and then lead a Diamond. One of the opponents will win it, and seeing that you are trying to trump a loser in dummy, may decide to lead a trump. You can win with dummy's Queen and lead another Diamond. Now East can win this trick and finish you off by leading the remaining Heart. You can win this one in your hand to lead your last Diamond, but there is no trump left in the dummy! You won't make your contract.

Instead, you must give up a Diamond trick as soon as you win the Ace of Spades. If the opponents lead a trump, you can win it in dummy and give up another Diamond trick. If they lead another trump, you can win it in your hand and you still have a Heart left in dummy with which to trump your last Diamond.

Here is a more difficult example:

Contract: Four Spades

West leads ♣K

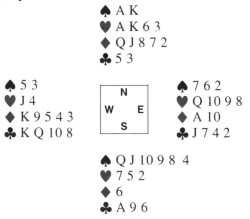

You can afford three losers. You have one Heart loser, one Diamond loser and two Club losers. There are no extra winners in the hand on which to throw a loser, but there is a doubleton Club in the dummy and you could plan to trump one of your Club losers.

The King of Clubs has been led. Let's suppose you take the Ace and play another Club, which the opponents win. Seeing that you plan to trump your Club loser in dummy, the opponents lead a trump that you win with a high Spade in the dummy. You would like to get back to your hand to trump the third Club, but you have no entry! You can play a Diamond, planning to trump the next round of Diamonds to reach your hand, but it will be too late. The opponents will win the Diamond and play another trump so that there are no Spades left in dummy to trump the third Club.

What could you do this time? It looks like you took your losses early by losing a Club trick as soon as you won the Ace . . . but it wasn't early enough. Instead, consider the difference if you let the opponents win the first Club with the King. Now, suppose they lead a trump to try to stop you from trumping your Club loser in dummy. You have to win it in the dummy, but you can get back to your hand with your carefully preserved Ace of Clubs. Then you can lead your remaining Club and trump it in dummy. The opponents can no longer stop you from making your contract.

By taking your losses very early, you kept a vital entry to your hand until you were ready to play it.

Summary

When you do not have enough tricks to make your contract, you often have to give up a trick to your opponents. You may need to do this to promote winners, establish long suits, take a finesse, discard a loser or trump losers in the dummy.

KEY MAXIM

Take Your Losses Early

You can only afford to give up a trick if you do not have too many quick losers. You must be able to regain the lead before the opponents can defeat your contract. To retain this control and to preserve any entries you might need, you should generally lose the necessary tricks at the earliest possible moment.

This does not mean that you should always lose your tricks immediately. You must try to lose them when the opponents can do you the least harm.

Exercises

1) You are in a contract of Four Hearts. Can you take your tricks and run or should you take your losses early?

♠ A K 2
♥ 8 7 5 3
♦ K J 4
♣ A 5 2

West leads ♠J

```
      N
  W       E
      S
```

♠ 9 8 7
♥ A K Q J 9
♦ Q 8
♣ J 4 3

Solution

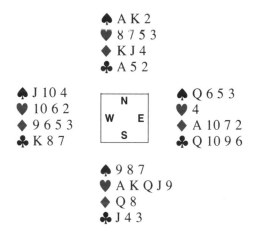

♠ A K 2
♥ 8 7 5 3
♦ K J 4
♣ A 5 2

♠ J 10 4   ♠ Q 6 5 3
♥ 10 6 2   ♥ 4
♦ 9 6 5 3   ♦ A 10 7 2
♣ K 8 7   ♣ Q 10 9 6

♠ 9 8 7
♥ A K Q J 9
♦ Q 8
♣ J 4 3

You can afford three losers. You have one Spade, one Diamond and two Clubs—one loser too many. You can't trump any of your losers in dummy, but you may be able to discard one on an extra winner in dummy. By driving out the opponents' Ace of Diamonds, dummy will have an extra winner.

Since you have too many losers, you cannot take your tricks and run. You do not have too many quick losers if you give up a trick to the opponents, since you still have a winner in every suit. Therefore, take your losses early. After winning the first Spade trick, you should play enough Heart tricks to eliminate the opponents' trump, then you should lose the Diamond trick that you have to lose immediately.

You do not have any entry problems on this hand, but you should still follow the basic principle of leading the high card from the short hand. Start with the Queen of Diamonds. You can play your small Diamond to dummy's King next. Once the opponents take their Ace, you can discard one of your losers on dummy's Jack.

2) You are in a contract of Three No Trump. How do you plan to make it?

♠ K 9 3
♥ Q J 5
♦ 10 7 4 3
♣ A 10 8

West leads ♥10

```
      N
  W       E
      S
```

♠ A Q 7
♥ A K 6
♦ 8 6 5 2
♣ K 9 4

Solution

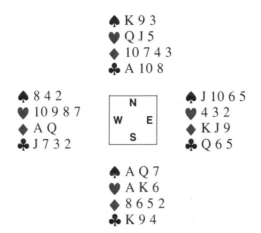

<pre>
                    ♠ K 9 3
                    ♥ Q J 5
                    ♦ 10 7 4 3
                    ♣ A 10 8

        ♠ 8 4 2   N   ♠ J 10 6 5
        ♥ 10 9 8 7   ♥ 4 3 2
        ♦ A Q   W   E   ♦ K J 9
        ♣ J 7 3 2   S   ♣ Q 6 5

                    ♠ A Q 7
                    ♥ A K 6
                    ♦ 8 6 5 2
                    ♣ K 9 4
</pre>

You need nine winners. You start with eight sure tricks: three Spades, three Hearts and two Clubs. Where will your ninth trick come from? The only source appears to be your long suit—Diamonds. You have eight Diamonds to the opponents' five. If the opponents' Diamonds break 3-2, you can give up three tricks to them, then finally establish a Diamond trick for yourself.

Entries are no problem because the suit is evenly divided. Nevertheless, you had better take your losses early! Don't start by taking your winners in the other suits, or you will merely establish tricks for your opponents. Win the first Heart trick and lead a Diamond. Win whatever they return and lead another Diamond. Win whatever they return . . . and so on, to make your contract.

3) Once again you are in Three No Trump. The opponents have started to knock out dummy's entries. Can you still make the contract?

         ♠ A K
         ♥ 7 6 2
         ♦ 10 4 3
         ♣ A 9 7 4 2

West leads ♠J

	N	
W		E
	S	

         ♠ Q 6 4 2
         ♥ A K 8
         ♦ A K 7
         ♣ 10 5 3

Solution

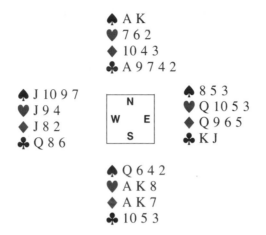

♠ A K
♥ 7 6 2
♦ 10 4 3
♣ A 9 7 4 2

♠ J 10 9 7
♥ J 9 4
♦ J 8 2
♣ Q 8 6

♠ 8 5 3
♥ Q 10 5 3
♦ Q 9 6 5
♣ K J

♠ Q 6 4 2
♥ A K 8
♦ A K 7
♣ 10 5 3

You need nine tricks and start with eight: three Spades, two Hearts, two Diamonds and one Club. Your only source for a ninth trick is the Club suit. You can hope that the opponents' Clubs are divided 3-2, and plan to establish a couple of small Clubs as winners in the dummy.

You must watch your entries to the dummy. If you win the Ace of Spades and play the Ace of Clubs followed by a small Club, the opponents will win and lead another Spade. You can win in dummy and lead Clubs once again to establish the suit, but your winners will be stranded.

Instead, you must win the Spade, then play a small Club from each hand to lose the trick. When the opponents play another Spade, you win in dummy. Again, you must be careful. You can't play the Ace and then give up a Club trick, because your winners would still be stranded. You must play, again, a small Club from each hand. Now you are in control. You can win whatever the opponents lead back and play your last Club to dummy's Ace. You are in dummy at the right moment to take your two Club winners and make a well deserved overtrick on this hand.

7

Get the Kiddies Off the Street

One of the first sayings you are likely to hear when you start to play bridge is **don't forget to draw trump**. This maxim goes back to the days when the game of whist, a forerunner of bridge, was a popular pastime. Whist was a gambling game, and there is a story told about the hundreds of players who walked the streets of London, penniless, without food or lodging, because they failed to draw trump. To increase the drama and to emphasize the importance of drawing trump, the story goes on to say that even the children and grandchildren of these players had to beg money for a cup of coffee. The saying is often interpreted as a rule with no exception—immediately draw all the trump you can afford. In many countries this rule is referred to as **get the kiddies off the street**.

When you are playing in a suit contract, a key decision is whether or not to lead trump. If you improve your judgement in this area, your game will get better by leaps and bounds. Proper management of the trump suit is often the characteristic that distinguishes the good player from the rest.

While it is true that drawing trump is often a good idea, there are times when you cannot do it immediately and even times when you do not do it at all. How do you know when to get the kiddies off the street? Once again, the secret is to make your plan. You'll have to determine whether or not you have too many losers and, if you do, whether they are quick losers or slow losers.

Let's see how all this works, starting off with what it means to **draw trump**.

Drawing Trump

How does having a trump suit affect the play of the hand? The difference between play in a No Trump contract and play in a suit contract is that the trump suit has greater trick-taking potential than the other suits. In No Trump, the highest card played in the suit that is led wins the trick. In a trump contract this is still true . . . unless a trump, regardless of its size, is played. The trump suit, then, becomes very important. You can use it to control the opponents' long suits; they can use it to trump your high cards. It is like having a group of cards at large that are higher than the Aces in the other suits. You can see why management of the trump suit is usually the declarer's primary consideration.

If you elect to play in a trump contract, normally your side has the majority of the trump. Usually, you have at least eight trump cards between your combined hands and the opponents have five or fewer. Even though you have most of the trump, the opponents' trump represents a danger. If you try to take your winners in other suits, one of the opponents might become void in the suit and play a trump, giving you an additional loser.

That is why you generally want to draw trump by playing the trump suit until the opponents have none left. Let's look at an example in which Hearts are the trump suit:

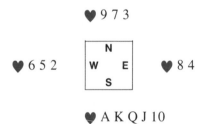

There is a total of thirteen cards in the suit. If you and your partner have eight, then the opponents have five. It is easier to think in terms of this smaller number when keeping track of how much trump you have to draw. When you play the Ace, you see two trumps played by the opponents, leaving three more. When you play the King, you see another two trumps played by the opponents, leaving one outstanding. When you play the Queen, the opponents' last trump will appear. You have now drawn trump.

It may take more than three rounds to draw the opponents' trump even when you have eight of them. For example, suppose the trump suit is divided in this fashion:

When you play the Ace, you again see two trumps played, leaving three outstanding. On the King you see only one trump played by your opponents because East has no more and will have to discard a card from another suit. That leaves two trump outstanding. You will have to play both your Queen and Jack to extract all of the opponents' trump. If one of your opponents had discarded when you played the first round of trump, the trump would be divided 5-0 and you would have to play all five of your Hearts to completely draw trump.

When drawing trump, you may have to give up the lead to your opponents:

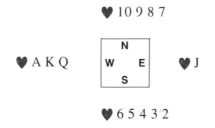

You may not be pleased with the look of this trump suit, but you can still draw trump. You have nine trump cards, so the opponents have four. When you lead the suit, two of the opponents' trump appear. When you get in again, you can continue to lead trump. They will end up winning three trump tricks but you will have drawn trump. Your remaining two trump cards will be winners and there will no longer be any danger that the opponents can trump one of your winners in another suit. If you had not drawn trump, the opponents might have taken four trump tricks: East might have trumped a trick with his Jack and West still would have had the Ace, King and Queen left.

The suit might even be more favorably divided:

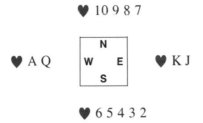

♥ 10 9 8 7

♥ A Q   ♥ K J

♥ 6 5 4 3 2

Now, when you lead the suit the first time, two of the opponents' trumps appear. When you get an opportunity to lead the suit again, both the remaining trump cards fall together. You have now drawn trump and only lost two tricks, even though the opponents had the four highest cards in the trump suit.

When You Do Not Have Too Many Losers

The most common situation in which you draw trump right away is when you don't have any losers to eliminate. Let's see how this works in a complete hand:

Contract: Four Spades

West leads ♥ K

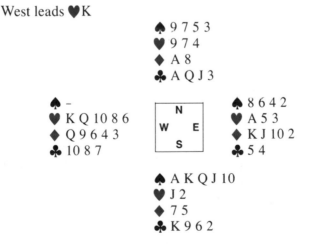

♠ 9 7 5 3
♥ 9 7 4
♦ A 8
♣ A Q J 3

♠ -
♥ K Q 10 8 6
♦ Q 9 6 4 3
♣ 10 8 7

♠ 8 6 4 2
♥ A 5 3
♦ K J 10 2
♣ 5 4

♠ A K Q J 10
♥ J 2
♦ 7 5
♣ K 9 6 2

You can afford three losers. You have two Heart losers and one Diamond loser. Since there are no losers to eliminate you should plan to draw the opponents' trump as soon as you take the lead.

Suppose the opponents win the first two Heart tricks, then play a third round, which you trump with your Ten of Spades. Your plan is to draw all of the opponents' trump right away. You have nine Spades—the opponents have four. When you lead the Ace of Spades, West discards a Diamond, so you know that East has all four trumps. What should you do now? It may seem wasteful to spend two of your trumps to get only one from the opponents. Yet even though you have to play the Ace, King, Queen and Jack—all of your trump cards—you must still get the kiddies off the street. Once you have done so, you can take your four Club winners and the Ace of Diamonds to make your contract.

What if you had ignored the saying and started to play your Club winners first? East would follow suit in the first two rounds, but on the third round he would play one of his small trumps on your Club winner and you would end up with a loser you hadn't counted on. You would lose this trick plus the two Heart tricks and a Diamond trick and be defeated in a contract you could have made. You might have to join those whist players who walk the streets of London!

When you have decided that drawing trump right away is the best plan, don't forget to watch your entries:

Contract: Four Spades

West leads ♥Q

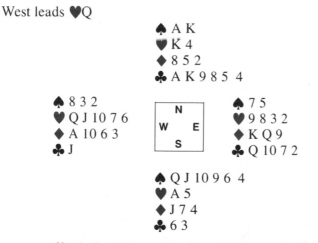

You can afford three losers and you have only three losers, all in Diamonds. Since you do not have more losers than you can afford, you plan to draw trump. Nevertheless, you must be careful. The opening lead is the Queen of Hearts and, on this hand, the card you play on the first trick will determine the success or failure of your contract.

Suppose you play the Four of Hearts from dummy and win the first trick with the Ace of Hearts in your hand. Now you start to draw trump. You have eight; the opponents have five. You play a small Spade from your hand and win the trick with a high Spade in dummy. Both opponents follow suit. There are three trump cards outstanding. You play your other high Spade from dummy and again both opponents follow suit. There is only one trump left to draw. Unfortunately, you are in the dummy and have no immediate entry to get back to your hand.

Your only hope to create an entry is to play the Ace and the King of Clubs, then try to trump a third round of Clubs in your hand. Look what happens, though, when you attempt this strategy: West ruffs the second Club with a small trump and you lose a trick you cannot afford.

What could you do to avoid this result? Drawing trump was an excellent idea, but you needed an entry to your hand to finish the job. In Chapter Three, we discussed the importance of keeping an entry to a long suit. In this case, the same principle applies, the long suit being the trump suit. Win the first trick with dummy's King of Hearts. Now, after playing dummy's Ace and King of Spades, you can come back safely to your hand with the Ace of Hearts to draw the remaining trump. You end up losing only the three Diamond tricks.

It is easy to confuse drawing trump with taking your tricks and running. Sometimes, when you have the number of losers you can afford and have decided to draw the trump, you have to give up the lead two or three times in order to do it.

Contract: Two Spades

West leads ♦ Q

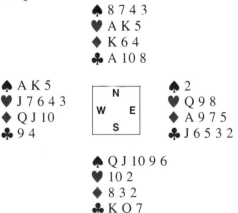

```
                        ♠ 8 7 4 3
                        ♥ A K 5
                        ♦ K 6 4
                        ♣ A 10 8

    ♠ A K 5                                 ♠ 2
    ♥ J 7 6 4 3          N                  ♥ Q 9 8
    ♦ Q J 10        W         E             ♦ A 9 7 5
    ♣ 9 4               S                   ♣ J 6 5 3 2

                        ♠ Q J 10 9 6
                        ♥ 10 2
                        ♦ 8 3 2
                        ♣ K Q 7
```

You can afford five losers. You have two Spade losers and three Diamond losers, for a total of five. If you leave a trump card at large you could develop an extra loser needlessly, so you must draw the trump.

West has led the Queen of Diamonds. You can try winning a trick with dummy's King, but it won't work on this hand. East has the Ace of Diamonds and the opponents win the first three tricks. Suppose they then lead a Club or a Heart and you win the trick. It may seem difficult to give the lead up again so soon, but it is valuable advice. Play a Spade. West wins the trick. Whatever he leads, you can win, then play another Spade. Again West wins the trick, but, whatever he returns, you can win and draw West's last trump. You have lost three Diamonds and two Spades, but you make your contract.

Don't be reluctant to draw trump even if it means giving up the lead. Look at the above hand and see what would have happened if you had tried to take your winners before drawing all of the opponents' trumps. You would lose an extra trick needlessly when the opponents trumped one of your winners.

This concept is further illustrated in the following hand:

Contract: Four Spades

West leads ♥10

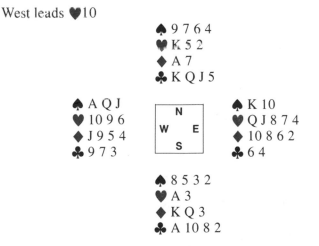

When the Ten of Hearts is led and you see dummy for the first time, you may be disappointed by that anemic trump suit. In your disappointment, you may be tempted to play a suit that will give you an instant feeling of success, such as the Clubs. What happens when you play the third round of the Club suit? East wins the trick by trumping with the Ten of Spades and the opponents still hold the Ace, King, Queen and Jack.

How can you prevent this outcome? You can afford three losers. Your only losers are in the trump suit and, if the Spades are divided 3-2, you should only have to lose three trump tricks. Draw trump.

When you win the opening lead, play a Spade. The opponents will win the trick and lead another suit. Play another Spade. Again the opponents win the trick, but whatever they lead back, you are now in control. There is only one high Spade outstanding and that is the only trick you have left to lose.

When You Have Too Many Losers

Thus far, we have looked at hands in which you can afford the number of losers that you have. Drawing trump is always a good idea in that situation. However, in most hands you will have too many losers. Drawing trump as soon as you get the lead may still be a good idea, but you will have to consider whether that puts the contract at risk.

You must first determine if your losers are quick or slow. If they are slow, drawing trump will not put the contract in jeopardy provided you do not need the trump for some other purpose (such as trumping losers). If the losers are quick, you have to decide if drawing trump will give the opponents the lead before you have had a chance to eliminate your losers. Let's look at some examples.

Contract: Six Spades

West leads ♣K

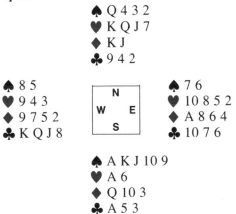

You can afford only one loser. You have three—one Diamond and two Clubs—so there are two losers to eliminate. You have two extra winners in the Heart suit, so you could plan to discard your two Club losers there.

How do you put it all together? Will drawing trump put the contract at risk? Once the King of Clubs is led and you take the Ace, you have three quick losers if the opponents get the lead. In this case, your trump suit is solid—you won't have to give up the lead when drawing trump. Therefore, start by getting the kiddies off the street.

After playing the Ace and the King of Spades, the opponents have no trump left. Now you can stop drawing trump and eliminate your Club losers. Play the Ace of Hearts followed by the Six of Hearts to dummy's King. Then play the Queen and Jack of Hearts to discard your two losing Clubs. You are left with only one quick loser, the Ace of Diamonds. Lead the King of Diamonds to drive out the opponents' Ace and you will make your slam contract.

On this hand you have quick losers to eliminate, but drawing trump does not force you to give up the lead. If you do not draw trump on this hand, you won't make the contract because the opponents will trump one of your Heart winners and you will not be able to discard both of your Club losers.

Here's another hand:

Contract: Four Hearts

West leads ♣Q

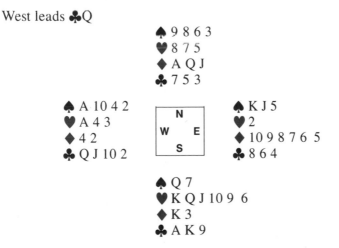

You can afford three losers. You have two Spade losers, one Heart loser and one Club loser—you have one loser too many. You also have an extra Diamond winner in dummy on which you can discard one of your losers. Should you draw trump?

After you win the opening lead with a high Club, you have three quick losers: two Spades and the Ace of Hearts. The fourth loser, the Club, is a slow loser. This means that you can afford to give up the lead while drawing trump because you do not have too many quick losers. The opponents can take only three tricks before you regain the lead. Once again, you can afford to draw trump before discarding your loser.

Win the first Club trick, then lead the King of Hearts to drive out the Ace. The opponents can take two Spade tricks, but then you can win whatever they lead next. Continue to draw their trump. On this hand, the distribution is 3-1; you will have to play two more rounds to get all the kiddies off the street. Now it is safe to play the Diamonds and take your discard. Play the King, followed by a small Diamond to the Ace. Lead your last high Diamond from dummy and discard your Nine of Clubs. You have taken care of all your losers, and you are left with nothing but trump winners.

When you have a loser to eliminate, there may be times when you can throw it on an extra winner, but sometimes you must trump it in the dummy. In order to do so, you must retain enough trump in the dummy to trump your losers.

Contract: Three Spades

West leads ♥4

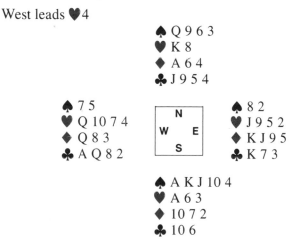

```
                    ♠ Q 9 6 3
                    ♥ K 8
                    ♦ A 6 4
                    ♣ J 9 5 4

    ♠ 7 5                          ♠ 8 2
    ♥ Q 10 7 4       N             ♥ J 9 5 2
    ♦ Q 8 3      W       E         ♦ K J 9 5
    ♣ A Q 8 2        S             ♣ K 7 3

                    ♠ A K J 10 4
                    ♥ A 6 3
                    ♦ 10 7 2
                    ♣ 10 6
```

You can afford four losers. With one Heart loser, two Diamond losers and two Club losers, you have one loser too many. You cannot eliminate your Club and Diamond losers, but you can plan to trump your Heart loser in the dummy because dummy has only two Hearts. Should you draw trump first?

You have two quick Club losers, but your other losers are slow. They present no problem and, on this hand, you can draw trump without giving up the lead to the opponents. Draw trump first, but remember to keep a trump in dummy in order to trump your Heart loser.

Win the first Heart with dummy's King. You want to keep the Ace of Hearts as an entry to your hand so that you can lead your small Heart and trump it in dummy. Now, you can start to draw trump. You have nine trumps; the opponents have four. When you lead the first round, both opponents follow suit . . . only two left. When you lead Spades again, the remaining two trumps appear. The trump is drawn and you can safely play the Ace of Hearts and trump your loser in dummy. You have no losers left to worry about.

Suppose the hand is slightly different:

Contract: Three Spades

West leads ♥4

```
                    ♠ Q 9 6 3
                    ♥ K 8
                    ♦ A 6 4
                    ♣ J 9 5 4

   ♠ 8 7 5 2            N            ♠ -
   ♥ Q 10 7 4      W         E       ♥ J 9 5 2
   ♦ Q 8                              ♦ K J 9 3 3
   ♣ A Q 8            S              ♣ K 7 3 2

                    ♠ A K J 10 4
                    ♥ A 6 3
                    ♦ 10 7 2
                    ♣ 10 6
```

As before, you win the first trick with dummy's King of Hearts, but this time, when you lead a trump, East discards a small Diamond. East's play indicates that the opponents' trump is divided 4-0. You will have to play four rounds of the suit to extract all of West's trump. If you do so, dummy will have no trump left with which to trump your Heart loser.

Clearly, you cannot afford to draw all the trump immediately. First you must play a Heart to your Ace, then lead your small Heart and trump it in dummy. Only then is it safe to draw the rest of West's trump to make your contract. (In the next chapter, we will look in more detail at hands in which you delay drawing trump.)

Summary

One of the oldest maxims in the game is draw trump as soon as you can. If you don't follow this advice, you may find the opponents' trump turning up at the most inopportune times, interrupting your plan and creating extra losers you hadn't counted on.

KEY MAXIM

Get the Kiddies Off the Street
(Draw Trump)

This maxim tells you to play the trump suit at every opportunity until the opponents have none left. Yet, before deciding to draw trump, you should always make your plan. When you can afford the losers that you have, then get the kiddies off the street. If you have too many losers, you can still use this piece of advice, as long as: 1) you don't have to give up the lead while drawing trump and you don't need your trump for other purposes, 2) you have to give up the lead while drawing trump, but you don't have too many quick losers and don't need your trump for other purposes.

Exercises

1) Your contract is Four Spades. West plays the Ace and the King of Hearts, then leads the Eight of Diamonds. Make your plan, keeping in mind the maxim—get the kiddies off the street—and decide how you would play this hand.

♠ K 8 5
♥ Q 7
♦ A Q 7 6
♣ A J 7 5

West leads ♥A

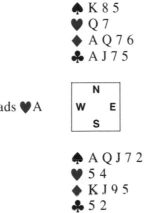

♠ A Q J 7 2
♥ 5 4
♦ K J 9 5
♣ 5 2

Solution

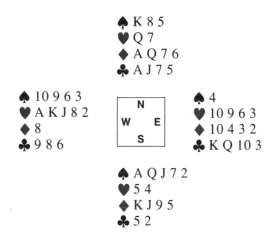

♠ K 8 5
♥ Q 7
♦ A Q 7 6
♣ A J 7 5

♠ 10 9 6 3
♥ A K J 8 2
♦ 8
♣ 9 8 6

♠ 4
♥ 10 9 6 3
♦ 10 4 3 2
♣ K Q 10 3

♠ A Q J 7 2
♥ 5 4
♦ K J 9 5
♣ 5 2

You can afford three losers. You have two Heart losers and one Club loser. You don't have more losers than you can afford; therefore, you should plan to draw trump.

After West takes the first two Heart tricks, then leads a Diamond, you should win the Diamond and immediately start to draw trump. You can start with the King of Spades (high card from the short side) and continue by leading a Spade to your Ace. When the trump breaks 4-1, you must lead your Queen and Jack to extract all of West's trump. You can then take your remaining winners in peace.

As you can see in the actual hand, if you play another Diamond before drawing all the trump, West will trump it and defeat your contract.

2) You reach a contract of Six Hearts. It looks as though you will have little difficulty in making your contract, but what if the opponents' trump divides 4-0?

♠ K 8
♥ A K Q
♦ A 7 6 4 2
♣ A K Q

West leads ♠J

```
      N
 W         E
      S
```

♠ A 6
♥ J 8 5 4 3 2
♦ Q 5
♣ J 5 4

Solution

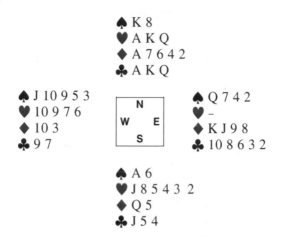

♠ K 8
♥ A K Q
♦ A 7 6 4 2
♣ A K Q

♠ J 10 9 5 3
♥ 10 9 7 6
♦ 10 3
♣ 9 7

♠ Q 7 4 2
♥ –
♦ K J 9 8
♣ 10 8 6 3 2

♠ A 6
♥ J 8 5 4 3 2
♦ Q 5
♣ J 5 4

You can afford one loser, and it appears that one Diamond loser is all you have. You want to draw trump, but be careful! Make sure you win the opening lead in dummy with the King of Spades. You may need the Ace of Spades as an entry to your hand.

On this hand, when you win the lead and play the Ace of Hearts, East discards a Club. Now you know that West started with all four trump cards. Take the King and the Queen of Hearts, then use your Ace of Spades as an entry to draw the remaining trump with your Jack of Hearts. From there on, it's clear sailing and you can take your remaining winners.

Take a look and see what happens if you win the first Spade trick in your hand. You'll find that you can't get back to your hand to draw the last trump and you will end up losing both a Diamond trick and a Heart trick.

3) You are in a contract of Four Spades. How do you plan to play the contract?

        ♠ Q J 8 7
        ♥ Q 9 3
        ♦ A 9 3
        ♣ A K 8

West leads ♦ J

        ♠ 10 9 6 5 3
        ♥ K J 2
        ♦ K Q 2
        ♣ 7 5

Solution

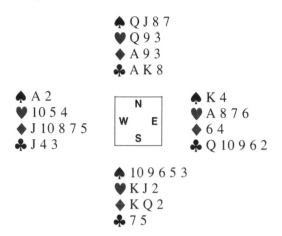

♠ Q J 8 7
♥ Q 9 3
♦ A 9 3
♣ A K 8

♠ A 2
♥ 10 5 4
♦ J 10 8 7 5
♣ J 4 3

♠ K 4
♥ A 8 7 6
♦ 6 4
♣ Q 10 9 6 2

♠ 10 9 6 5 3
♥ K J 2
♦ K Q 2
♣ 7 5

You can afford three losers, which is exactly what you have: three sure losses to the Ace and the King of Spades and the Ace of Hearts. When you put it all together, your first priority is to get the kiddies off the street. Yet, because you will have to give up the lead in order to draw trump, you must check that you don't have too many quick losers. In this hand, you have only three quick losers—so get to work.

Since entries are no problem, win the first Diamond in either hand and lead a trump to drive out the opponents' King. Whatever they return, win it and lead another trump to drive out the Ace. When the trump divides 2-2, all your troubles are over. You can now drive out the Ace of Hearts and make your contract.

It looks easy enough, but, if you don't draw trump, East will trump the third Diamond trick with the Four of Spades and you will end up with four losers.

8

Get the Kiddies Off the Street . . .
The Other Side of the Coin

In the last chapter we saw that drawing the opponents' trump as soon as possible is usually a good idea. There are times, however, when declarer must delay drawing trump and attend to more pressing concerns.

How does declarer know if there are priorities higher than drawing trump? The answer comes when you make your plan. In the previous chapter you saw that you should draw trump when:

- You don't have too many losers
- You don't have to give up the lead while drawing trump and don't need your trump for other purposes
- You have to give up the lead while drawing trump, but you don't have too many quick losers and don't need your trump for other purposes.

In this chapter, we'll look at some of the situations in which you cannot afford to draw all of the opponents' trump right away:

- You have too many quick losers, so you can't draw trump if it means giving up the lead before you have a chance to dispose of your losers
- You need to trump losers in the dummy
- You have entry problems
- You need trump to maintain control of the opponents' suits

135

Eliminating Quick Losers

If the trump suit is not solid, the opponents will win one or more tricks when you draw trump. Sometimes you cannot afford to let the opponents have the lead because they will immediately be able to take enough tricks to defeat your contract. If you have too many quick losers, you must dispose of them before giving up the lead to the opponents. This is one reason to delay drawing trump.

Look at this example:

Contract: Four Spades

West leads ♣Q

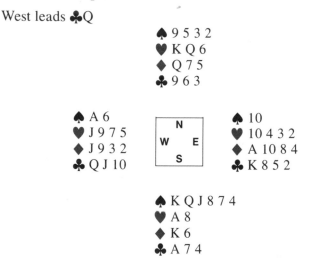

```
              ♠ 9 5 3 2
              ♥ K Q 6
              ♦ Q 7 5
              ♣ 9 6 3

 ♠ A 6                        ♠ 10
 ♥ J 9 7 5      N             ♥ 10 4 3 2
 ♦ J 9 3 2    W   E           ♦ A 10 8 4
 ♣ Q J 10       S             ♣ K 8 5 2

              ♠ K Q J 8 7 4
              ♥ A 8
              ♦ K 6
              ♣ A 7 4
```

You can afford three losers. You have a Spade loser, a Diamond loser and two Club losers. You have an extra Heart winner in dummy so you can plan to discard one of your losers on it.

Should you get the kiddies off the street first? No, you have too many quick losers. To draw trump you have to give up a trick to the opponents' Ace. They will then be in a position to take four tricks and defeat your contract. Delay drawing trump and play three rounds of Hearts, then discard one of your Club losers. Now, start drawing the trump, because when the opponents take the trick with their Ace, they can no longer defeat the contract.

Here is a more subtle example:

Contract: Four Hearts

West leads ♠J

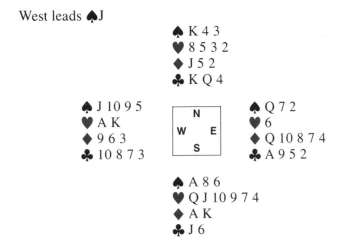

♠ K 4 3
♥ 8 5 3 2
♦ J 5 2
♣ K Q 4

♠ J 10 9 5
♥ A K
♦ 9 6 3
♣ 10 8 7 3

♠ Q 7 2
♥ 6
♦ Q 10 8 7 4
♣ A 9 5 2

♠ A 8 6
♥ Q J 10 9 7 4
♦ A K
♣ J 6

Once again, you can afford three losers. You have a Spade loser, two Heart losers and a Club loser. You can't avoid losses to the Ace and the King of Hearts or the Ace of Clubs—they are quick losers—the opponents can take them when they get the lead. Plan, therefore, to eliminate your Spade loser. You can't trump it in dummy and don't have any immediate sure tricks on which to discard it. However, you can establish an extra Club winner in dummy by driving out the opponents' Ace, which will give you an extra trick on which to discard your Spade.

Can you start drawing trump? To establish the extra Club winner, you must give up the lead to the opponents. You can afford to do this once; because your Spade loser is slow, they can't immediately take a Spade trick. To draw trump, you also have to give up the lead to the opponents. If you do so, the opponents may lead another Spade. You will have no high cards left in Spades and your remaining Spade is a quick loser. You can't discard it because you have not yet established the extra Club winner in dummy, and you can't establish the extra winner because you would have to give up the lead to the opponents.

Since you will have to let the opponents in when you draw trump, you cannot afford to draw trump right away on this hand. You must carefully win the first Spade trick in your hand, making sure you preserve the King of Spades as an entry to the dummy. Next you lead the Jack of Clubs, high card from the short side, to start to establish the extra Club winner. If the opponents don't play their Ace, lead the suit again to drive it out. Now they must take it or you will end up with no Club loser. If they lead back a Spade, win it in dummy with your carefully preserved King, then play your established Club winner and discard a Spade on it. Now it is safe to start drawing the opponents' trump because you have only three losers.

Trumping Losers in the Dummy

There are times when you have too many losers and the only way to eliminate some of them is by trumping them in dummy. As we saw in the last chapter, if you have plenty of trump, you can afford to draw the opponents' trump first and still have enough left over to trump your losers. Sometimes, however, your situation is not so comfortable.

Contract: Four Spades

West leads ♣Q

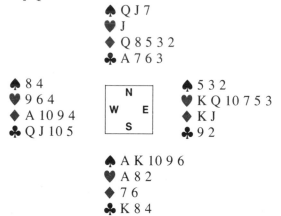

You can afford three losers. You have two Heart losers, two Diamond losers and a Club loser, for a total of five. There are no extra winners in dummy on which to discard your losers and it would be difficult to establish any. Instead, look for an opportunity to trump your losers in the dummy. The singleton Heart in dummy provides the possibility of trumping both of your Heart losers.

Can you draw trump first? You need two trump cards in the dummy to take care of your Heart losers and, since it will take at least three rounds to draw all of the opponents' trump, you cannot afford to draw trump.

You will need entries to your hand in order to lead your Heart losers and trump them in dummy, so win the first trick with dummy's Ace of Clubs, keeping the King in your hand. You can now play the Ace of Hearts and then trump one of your Heart losers in dummy. You can use the King of Clubs as an entry back to your hand to lead your remaining Heart loser and trump it in dummy. Once you have eliminated your extra losers, you can start to draw trump.

Let's look at another example:

Contract: Four Spades

West leads ♦K

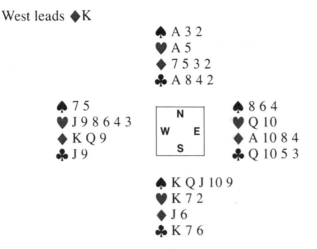

               ♠ A 3 2
               ♥ A 5
               ♦ 7 5 3 2
               ♣ A 8 4 2

♠ 7 5   ♠ 8 6 4
♥ J 9 8 6 4 3   ♥ Q 10
♦ K Q 9   ♦ A 10 8 4
♣ J 9   ♣ Q 10 5 3

               ♠ K Q J 10 9
               ♥ K 7 2
               ♦ J 6
               ♣ K 7 6

Once again, you can afford three losers. You have four losers: a Heart, two Diamonds and one Club. You can't eliminate the two Diamond losers, because the defenders are about to take the first two Diamond tricks. There is nowhere to discard your Club loser. Therefore, you plan to trump your Heart loser in the dummy.

Suppose the opponents start off by playing the King and the Queen of Diamonds, followed by another Diamond, which you trump. Can you afford to draw all of the opponents' trump? They have five trump cards, so even if they break 3-2, you would have to play three rounds. You could afford to play two rounds before trumping your loser, leaving one trump in dummy, but in order to illustrate another interesting twist to this hand, let's assume you decide to trump your loser before drawing any trump.

You play a Heart to dummy's Ace and a Heart back to your King. Then you lead your remaining Heart and trump it in dummy. Which of dummy's trumps did you use? On this hand, if you try to trump your loser with one of dummy's small trumps, East will **over-trump** by playing a higher trump, since he is also out of Hearts—an unfortunate turn of events because you can no longer make your contract.

To prevent this outcome, trump your loser with your high trump, the Ace. East cannot over-trump this card. Draw the opponents' trump and you will make your contract. On this hand, you can afford to play it safe by trumping with one of your high trump since you still have enough high cards left to draw the opponents' trump. You won't always have this luxury, but when you do, don't fall into the trap of sending a boy to do a man's job . . . or is it a girl to do a woman's job?

If you decide to draw two rounds of trump on this hand before trumping your Heart loser, be careful to leave dummy's Ace as the remaining trump.

Watching Entries

The trump suit itself can often be useful as a source of entries between declarer and dummy. Sometimes, you have to combine drawing trump with a judicious use of your entries. Look at this example:

Contract: Two Hearts

West leads ♦10

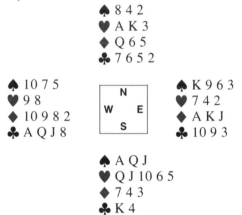

```
            ♠ 8 4 2
            ♥ A K 3
            ♦ Q 6 5
            ♣ 7 6 5 2
♠ 10 7 5                  ♠ K 9 6 3
♥ 9 8          N          ♥ 7 4 2
♦ 10 9 8 2  W     E       ♦ A K J
♣ A Q J 8      S          ♣ 10 9 3
            ♠ A Q J
            ♥ Q J 10 6 5
            ♦ 7 4 3
            ♣ K 4
```

You can afford five losers. You have a Spade loser because you are missing the King, three Diamond losers and two Club losers, for a total of six. West leads a Diamond and East takes the first three Diamond tricks. East now leads a Club and you try to win a trick with your King, but West plays the Ace and then takes a trick with the Queen. West leads another Club and, finally, you win a trick by trumping it in your hand.

You have already lost five tricks; if you are going to make your contract, you will have to avoid losing a Spade trick. Is there any way to do so? Yes: you must hope that East has the King and try a finesse.

Can you afford to draw trump first? The problem in this hand is that you must lead a Spade from dummy to take a finesse. In fact, if the finesse works, you must get back to dummy to do it again to avoid losing a trick to East's King. Your only entries to dummy are in the trump suit, so you cannot afford to use them up too soon. Let's see what you have to do.

Start drawing trump by playing a small trump to dummy's Ace. Now that you are in dummy, use the entry to play a Spade toward your hand. When East plays a low Spade, try a finesse by playing the Jack (or Queen). You will win the trick if West doesn't have the King. But now you are in your hand. Play a small trump to dummy's King and use this entry to lead another Spade toward your hand. When East plays a low card, repeat the finesse by playing your Queen (or Jack). When you win, you can draw the remaining trump and play your Ace of Spades to make your contract.

Here is a similar example, but this time, the problem is in the trump suit itself.

Contract: Four Spades

West leads ♥Q

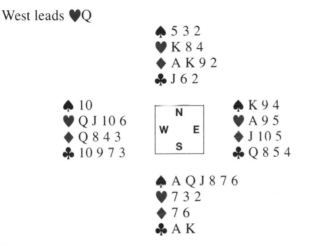

After West's lead, the opponents take the first three Heart tricks. They lead a Club and you win it in your hand. You can only afford three losers and have already lost them. You still have a potential loser in Spades because you are missing the King. To avoid losing a Spade trick, you will have to try a finesse, as in the previous example.

Once again, you can't play your trump suit right away. You are in your hand and need to be in the dummy to take a finesse. You will have to delay drawing trump and play a small Diamond over to dummy's Ace. Now you can start drawing trump by leading a Spade toward your hand and finessing the Jack (or Queen). When this works, stop drawing trump for a moment and play your remaining Diamond to dummy's King. Then you can lead another trump toward your hand and repeat the finesse. There is only one trump left outstanding, the King. You can play your Ace and draw it. The rest of the tricks are yours.

Maintaining Control

One of the advantages of having a trump suit is that you can trump the opponents' winners once you have no cards left in a suit. However, this move is possible only if you have some trump left. On some hands you must be careful not to run out of trump cards by playing too many too early. Here is an example:

Contract: Four Hearts

West leads ♦J

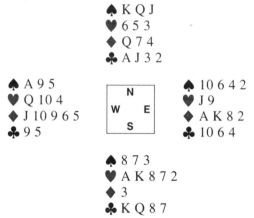

```
                    ♠ K Q J
                    ♥ 6 5 3
                    ♦ Q 7 4
                    ♣ A J 3 2

 ♠ A 9 5                             ♠ 10 6 4 2
 ♥ Q 10 4          N                 ♥ J 9
 ♦ J 10 9 6 5   W     E              ♦ A K 8 2
 ♣ 9 5             S                 ♣ 10 6 4

                    ♠ 8 7 3
                    ♥ A K 8 7 2
                    ♦ 3
                    ♣ K Q 8 7
```

You can afford three losers. You will definitely lose a Spade and a Diamond trick. In the Heart suit, you will have to hope that the opponents' trump is divided 3-2, so that you only have to lose one trick. You plan to play the Ace and the King and, if both opponents follow suit each time, there will only be one trump card outstanding. Even though it is higher than your remaining trump, it is your only remaining loser.

Suppose the opponents win the first Diamond trick and play another Diamond, which you trump with your Two of Hearts. Since you won't have too many losers if the trump breaks, you can draw trump. You play the Ace and the King and fortunately, the trump divides nicely as both opponents follow suit. What now?

Look what happens if you get carried away by getting the kiddies off the street. You play another trump and West wins the Queen. All the opponents' trump is gone, but you only have one left. If West leads another Diamond, you will have to use your last trump to win the trick. You still have to drive out the opponents' Ace of Spades to establish your Spade winners. When West wins the Ace, he leads more Diamonds and, since you have no trump left, the Diamonds are winners. You end up having to discard some of your winners on West's Diamonds and you don't make your contract. You lost control of the hand.

How could you prevent this loss from happening? It is a good idea to play the Ace and the King of Hearts to draw the opponents' small trump, but you should stop there. At this point, you have two small trump cards left in your hand and one small trump left in dummy. The only outstanding trump is the Queen, one of your losers. You do not have to play two of your trump cards to draw out this one card. It is a trick you have to lose, so let the opponents take it when they want. Instead, turn your attention to the work that has to be done and lead a Spade to drive out the opponents' Ace. West can win the Ace and play the Queen of Hearts to eliminate dummy's remaining trump and one of your trump cards. But now, when he leads another Diamond, you still have a trump left. You can win the trick and take all your remaining winners, making your contract.

You do not always have to draw all of the opponents' trump. If there is only one trump left and it is higher than your trump, you can usually leave it out there and go about establishing and playing your other winners. Keep your trump to retain control because, once all the trump is gone, the play becomes similar to No Trump: if the opponents get the lead, they can take all their winners.

There are some hands in which you never get around to drawing trump at all! Here is an example:

Contract: Four Spades

West leads ♥K

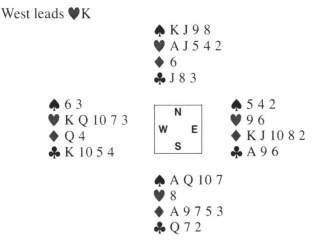

You can afford three losers. You have no losers in Spades and Hearts, but you have four potential Diamond losers and three potential Club losers.

That's seven losers. You will have to eliminate four of them. fortunately, dummy has a singleton Diamond. You can plan to trump all your Diamond losers in dummy.

Can you draw trump? You are going to need all of dummy's trump to trump your Diamond losers, so you cannot afford to play even one round. You can start by winning the Ace of Hearts, playing dummy's small Diamond to your Ace, then leading another Diamond and trumping it in dummy. But now what are you going to use as an entry back to your hand so that you can lead another Diamond?

The only way you can get back is by trumping one of dummy's Hearts. After doing this, you can lead another Diamond and trump it in dummy. Again, you must lead a Heart and trump it in your hand so that you can lead another Diamond loser and trump it in dummy. Continuing in this fashion, you lead another Heart from dummy and trump it in your hand. You lead your last Diamond and trump it in dummy with dummy's last trump. You can lead dummy's last Heart and trump it with your last trump, the Ace of Spades. You've taken the first ten tricks and never drawn a round of trump!

Because you trumped, or **ruffed**, losers in both hands, crossing back and forth, playing a hand in this manner is called a **cross-ruff**. A hand such as this is not too common, but it shows that you don't always get the kiddies off the street.

Summary

When you come to the final step in your plan—How do I put it all together?—one of your considerations is whether or not to draw trump. In the last chapter you saw when to get the kiddies off the street. In this chapter, we looked at the other side of the coin, at some of the situations when you have to delay drawing all of the opponents' trump:

- You have to give up the lead while drawing trump, but you have too many quick losers
- You need to trump losers in the dummy
- You have entry problems
- You need trump to maintain control of the opponents' suits.

In each case, the secret is to make your plan and execute it carefully.

Exercises

1) You are in Four Hearts. After winning the Ace of Spades, do you start drawing trump? If not, why not?

♠ 9 8 6
♥ Q J 8
♦ K Q J
♣ A K 7 6

West leads ♠K

```
      N
  W       E
      S
```

♠ A 5 2
♥ K 10 9 6 4 3
♦ 8 5
♣ Q 3

Solution

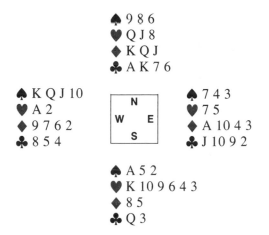

```
            ♠ 9 8 6
            ♥ Q J 8
            ♦ K Q J
            ♣ A K 7 6

♠ K Q J 10              ♠ 7 4 3
♥ A 2          N        ♥ 7 5
♦ 9 7 6 2   W     E     ♦ A 10 4 3
♣ 8 5 4        S        ♣ J 10 9 2

            ♠ A 5 2
            ♥ K 10 9 6 4 3
            ♦ 8 5
            ♣ Q 3
```

You can afford three losers. You have two Spade losers, a Heart loser and a Diamond loser—one loser too many. You cannot avoid the Heart and Diamond losers, but you can plan to discard one of your Spade losers on the extra Club winner in dummy.

To draw trump, you will have to give up a trick to the Ace. Once your Ace of Spades has been driven out, you will have four quick losers if the opponents get the lead. Thus, you cannot afford to draw trump right away. First you must discard one of your Spade losers. Win the Ace of Spades and play the Queen of Clubs, high card from the short side, and then a Club to dummy's Ace. Play dummy's King of Clubs and discard a small Spade from your hand. Now you can safely start to draw the opponents' trump.

2) You are in Four Spades. Should you draw trump right away or are there
other considerations?

♠ K 8 5
♥ A 9 8 2
♦ Q 7
♣ A 8 4 2

West leads ♣Q

```
      N
   W     E
      S
```

♠ A Q J 10 7 6
♥ J 3
♦ 9 6 3
♣ K 7

Solution

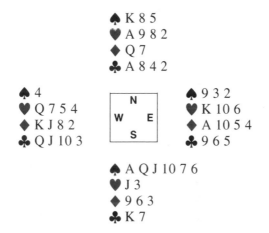

♠ K 8 5
♥ A 9 8 2
♦ Q 7
♣ A 8 4 2

♠ 4
♥ Q 7 5 4
♦ K J 8 2
♣ Q J 10 3

♠ 9 3 2
♥ K 10 6
♦ A 10 5 4
♣ 9 6 5

♠ A Q J 10 7 6
♥ J 3
♦ 9 6 3
♣ K 7

You can afford three losers. You have a Heart loser and three Diamond losers, for a total of four. There is nowhere to discard any of your losers, so you should look to see if you can trump some of them in the dummy. Since dummy has only two Diamonds, you can plan to trump one of your Diamond losers there.

Can you afford to draw trump? You will need to keep one trump card in the dummy with which to trump your loser. You have nine trump cards and the opponents have only four. If they are divided 2-2, you can draw them and still have one left in dummy. What if they are distributed 3-1 or 4-0? If you play two rounds of trump and then stop to try and trump your loser, it will be too late. You have to lose Diamond tricks to make dummy void, and when you do this, one of the opponents may be unkind enough to lead a trump and remove dummy's last trump.

Since you have to lose two Diamond tricks before you can trump your loser, you cannot afford to play even one round of trump. If you do so, the opponents might continue to lead trump each time they get the lead, and again, you will not have a trump left in dummy when it comes time to trump your last Diamond.

Instead, delay drawing trump and take your losses early. Win the opening lead with dummy's Ace of Clubs, keeping the King in your hand as an entry. Immediately give up a Diamond trick to the opponents. If they lead a trump, you can win and give up another Diamond trick. They can lead another trump, but you will win the race. There is still a trump left in dummy with which to trump your loser.

3) You are in a contract of Three Clubs. West leads the Jack of Spades and the opponents take the first three Spade tricks. Then they lead a Diamond. How do you plan to make your contract?

　　　　　　　　　　♠ Q 7 3
　　　　　　　　　　♥ 10 6 4 2
　　　　　　　　　　♦ 9 7 6 3
　　　　　　　　　　♣ A 3

West leads ♠J
```
      N
  W       E
      S
```

　　　　　　　　　　♠ 8 4 2
　　　　　　　　　　♥ A Q
　　　　　　　　　　♦ A 5
　　　　　　　　　　♣ K Q J 8 5 2

Solution

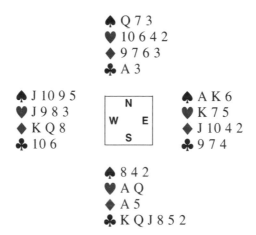

♠ Q 7 3
♥ 10 6 4 2
♦ 9 7 6 3
♣ A 3

♠ J 10 9 5
♥ J 9 8 3
♦ K Q 8
♣ 10 6

♠ A K 6
♥ K 7 5
♦ J 10 4 2
♣ 9 7 4

♠ 8 4 2
♥ A Q
♦ A 5
♣ K Q J 8 5 2

You can afford four losers. You have three Spade losers, a Diamond loser and a Heart loser. West leads the Jack of Spades. You can try to win a trick with dummy's Queen, but it won't work. You have to lose the three Spade tricks. Therefore, you must eliminate either the Diamond loser or the Heart loser. There is nowhere to discard either of them, nor can you trump them in dummy. However, you do have the Queen of Hearts and, if East has the King, you can make your contract by taking a finesse.

Should you draw trump first? To take the finesse, you need an entry to dummy. The only possible entry is the Ace of Clubs. If you draw trump right away, you will end up in your hand without an entry to dummy.

You must delay drawing all the trump. After winning the Ace of Diamonds, you can start drawing trump by leading a small Club to dummy's Ace. While you are in dummy, use the opportunity to lead a small Heart toward your hand. When East plays a small card, you play the Queen, which wins the trick. Having taken the finesse, now finish drawing the trump and you will make your contract.

9

Lead Toward the High Card
(The Finesse)

As you saw in Chapter One, a finesse is one of the common methods of developing an extra trick. It is an attempt to win a trick with a card that is ranked lower than one of those held by the opponents. Unlike building tricks through promotion, which always works when you have a sufficient number of high cards and entries, a finesse is not a sure thing. For success, you need a favorable position of particular cards in the opponents' hands.

There are many variations of the finesse, but the general principle can be summed by the popular maxim **lead toward the high card** . . . the card that you hope will take a trick. Let's see how we can put this saying to use.

Finessing Against the Ace

In Chapter One, we looked at the following position:

DUMMY: ♥ K 3

DECLARER: ♥ 5 2

To develop a trick in this suit, it does no good to lead from the dummy. If you lead the King, the opponents will win the trick with the Ace and then be in a position to take the rest of the tricks in the suit. If you lead the Three, the opponents will win the trick with a small card and then play the Ace, on which you must play the King. Again, they take all the tricks in the suit.

To have any hope for a trick, you must lead toward the high card. Play a small card from your hand toward the King and wait to see West's response. You hope that West has the Ace and the position resembles this:

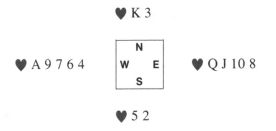

♥ K 3

♥ A 9 7 6 4   ♥ Q J 10 8

♥ 5 2

West must play a card before you choose the card you want to play from the dummy. If West plays the Ace, play dummy's Three and save your King for later. If West plays a small card, play dummy's King and it will win the trick because East doesn't have the Ace. This is the basic principle of the finesse . . . lead toward the card you hope will take a trick, in this case, the King.

Of course, the finesse depends on the favorable location of a particular card in the opponents' hands, which in this case is the Ace. The finesse is not a sure thing; the opponents' cards could be positioned in this manner:

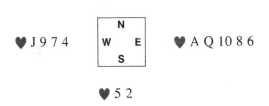

♥ K 3

♥ J 9 7 4   ♥ A Q 10 8 6

♥ 5 2

Play a small card from your hand, and when West plays a small card, play the King, hoping that West has the Ace. This time East has the Ace and you don't take a trick in the suit. It wouldn't have done any good to lead from dummy. No matter how you played the suit, you weren't destined to take a trick, but by leading toward the King, at least you gave yourself a chance.

The latter position illustrates the value of being able to play to a trick as late as possible. East, playing last, could wait to see which card you played from dummy before having to choose whether to play the Ace or win the trick with a smaller card. Look at the difference if East had to lead the suit. If he leads the Ace, you won't have to play the King and can save it to win the second trick. If East does not lead the Ace, you will win the first trick with your King. When East leads the suit you get to play last from the dummy. Unfortunately, the defenders won't often be kind enough to lead suits like this for you; you will have to do the work yourself . . . that's why you need a favorable position of the opponents' cards.

Now look at this position:

DUMMY: ♦ 7 5 3

DECLARER: ♦ K Q 6

You can develop one sure winner in this suit by leading the King from your hand to drive out the opponents' Ace, thereby promoting your Queen. However, suppose you need to take two tricks with these cards. Use the idea of the finesse . . . lead *toward* the high card. You might be able to develop two tricks. You will have to hope the Ace is favorably located, as in the following layout:

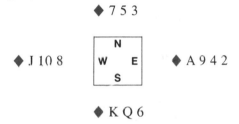

♦ 7 5 3

♦ J 10 8   ♦ A 9 4 2

♦ K Q 6

If East plays the Ace when you lead a small card from the dummy, play your Six, and both the King and the Queen are left as winners. If East plays a small card rather than the Ace, play your Queen (or King) and it will win the trick because West does not have the Ace. Now you are in a similar position to that in the earlier example:

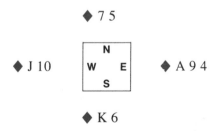

♦ 7 5

♦ J 10   ♦ A 9 4

♦ K 6

Go back to the dummy and lead toward your King. This is an example of a **repeated finesse** against the Ace. Of course, you must have enough entries to the dummy to be able to lead twice toward your hand. Remember to watch your entries.

Let's look at a full hand in which we are missing the Ace in a key suit:

Contract: Four Hearts

West leads ♦ K

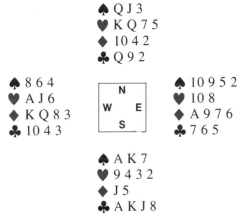

```
              ♠ Q J 3
              ♥ K Q 7 5
              ♦ 10 4 2
              ♣ Q 9 2

♠ 8 6 4          N          ♠ 10 9 5 2
♥ A J 6      W       E      ♥ 10 8
♦ K Q 8 3        S          ♦ A 9 7 6
♣ 10 4 3                    ♣ 7 6 5

              ♠ A K 7
              ♥ 9 4 3 2
              ♦ J 5
              ♣ A K J 8
```

West leads the King of Diamonds and continues with the Queen and a third round to East's Ace. You can trump with a small Heart. You can afford three losers, you have already lost two tricks and you are still missing the Ace of trump. You have no losers in the other suit, but will have to avoid losing more than one Heart trick.

Start by leading a Heart toward dummy. If West plays the Ace, your troubles are over. You can play a small card from dummy, and later use the King and the Queen to draw the rest of the opponents' trump. If West plays a small card, play the Queen (or King) from dummy. When it wins, you must come back to your hand with one of your entries, your Ace of Spades for example, and lead a Heart toward dummy's King. Whether West plays the Ace or a small card, you end up losing only one trump trick and you make your contract.

Finessing Against the King

In the first chapter, we looked at this position:

DUMMY: ♥ A Q 7
DECLARER: ♥ 4 2

You always have one trick, the Ace. If you need to develop two tricks, lead from your hand toward the dummy, hoping that West has the King. When West plays a small card, finesse dummy's Queen. If East doesn't have the King, your finesse will win.

As we saw earlier, sometimes you may have to repeat the finesse:

♠ A Q J

♠ K 9 6 3   ♠ 10 8 7 5

♠ 4 2

If you need three tricks from this suit, lead a small card from your hand toward dummy. When West plays small, finesse the Jack (or Queen). The finesse works, but now you are in the dummy. To repeat the finesse, you must have an entry back to your hand. Then lead your remaining small card toward dummy and take another finesse. Provided West started with the King, you will win all three tricks in the suit.

In the above examples, you have the Ace and the Queen in the same hand. With that combination, you don't have to lose a trick to the opponents' King. The position is a little different when the Ace and the Queen are in opposite hands.

DUMMY:	♥ A 8 4
DECLARER:	♥ Q 7 2

When your high cards are divided between the two hands, your holding is not as strong. You can no longer win two tricks without losing a trick to the opponents' King. But the principle of the finesse can still be applied. You lead toward the card you *hope* will take a trick. You know the Ace will take a trick, so the card you lead toward is the Queen, hoping that the opponents' cards are distributed like this:

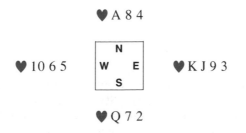

♥ A 8 4

♥ 10 6 5   ♥ K J 9 3

♥ Q 7 2

Lead the Four of Hearts from dummy. East has to play before you choose the card to play from your hand. If East plays the King, you can play a low card and your Queen will be a trick later. If East plays a little card, you play the Queen and it wins the trick. If East has the King, there is no way to prevent you taking two tricks. Notice, however, that if you had led the Queen originally, instead of leading toward it, East would win it with the King and you would only take one trick in the suit. Of course, the cards might not have been placed so favorably:

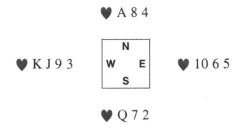

♥ A 8 4

♥ K J 9 3   ♥ 10 6 5

♥ Q 7 2

If this is the position, your finesse doesn't work. When you lead a small card from dummy and East plays a small card, you play your Queen, but West wins it with the King. Finesses don't always work. Notice, though, that it wouldn't have helped to lead the Queen originally. West would play the King on your Queen, making you use dummy's Ace to win the trick. The opponents would have the remaining high cards and you still would take only one trick.

In the previous example, since you were leading toward your Queen, it didn't matter whether or not you played your Ace first. In fact, you might use it as the entry to get to dummy and lead toward your Queen. It might even pay an unexpected benefit when one of the opponents has a singleton King. However, you cannot always afford to play the Ace first. Look at this position:

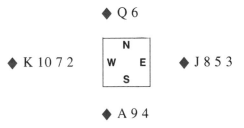

♦ Q 6

♦ K 10 7 2   ♦ J 8 5 3

♦ A 9 4

Suppose you need to take two winners from this suit. If you play the Ace first, you will have to also play dummy's Six. Dummy will be left with the singleton Queen. When you lead toward it, West will take the King and your Queen will have to be played. You will end up with only one trick. Instead, lead toward the Queen before playing your Ace. If West plays a small card, play dummy's Queen and win the trick. You will have the Ace left as a second trick. If West plays the King, play dummy's Six. Later you can take a trick with dummy's Queen and, when you get back to your hand, you can take a second trick with your Ace.

Here's a slightly different position:

♣ Q J 4 2

♣ K 10 9 8
```
      N
   W     E
      S
```
    ♣ 6 5

♣ A 7 3

You can always take two tricks in this suit, one with the Ace and one by using the Queen to drive out the opponents' King to establish your Jack. However, it would be nice to take three tricks. As long as West has the King, you should have no problem, now that you know about leading toward the high card. You know your Ace will take a trick, so you want to lead toward the cards you hope will win tricks: the Queen and the Jack.

Play a small card from your hand toward the dummy. If West plays the King, you will play dummy's Two. When you next get the lead, you will have three winners to take. If West plays a small card, play dummy's Jack (or Queen). You win the trick, but now you are in dummy. You can use the Ace to get back to your hand and play your remaining small card toward dummy's Queen. Whatever West plays, you will end up with three tricks.

In the above example, as long as West has the King, you can take three tricks. However, all may not be lost even if East has the King:

♣ Q J 4 2

♣ 9 6 5
```
      N
   W     E
      S
```
    ♣ K 10 8

♣ A 7 3

When you lead a small card to dummy's Jack (or Queen), East wins with the King. You still have two sure tricks. You can take the Ace and play your remaining small card to dummy's Queen. When the opponents' cards break 3-3, you end up with three tricks after all, since dummy's remaining small card is a winner.

Let's look at a variation on this theme in a complete hand:

Contract: Four Spades

West leads ♦ 4

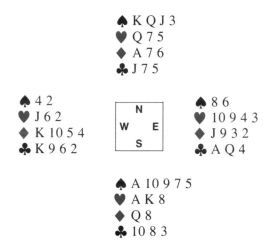

```
                  ♠ K Q J 3
                  ♥ Q 7 5
                  ♦ A 7 6
                  ♣ J 7 5

    ♠ 4 2           N            ♠ 8 6
    ♥ J 6 2                      ♥ 10 9 4 3
    ♦ K 10 5 4   W     E         ♦ J 9 3 2
    ♣ K 9 6 2       S            ♣ A Q 4

                  ♠ A 10 9 7 5
                  ♥ A K 8
                  ♦ Q 8
                  ♣ 10 8 3
```

You can afford three losers. It looks like you have four losers: three Clubs and a Diamond. There is nowhere to discard any of your losers and you can't trump any in dummy. Is there any hope?

You are missing the King of Diamonds, but you have the Queen in your hand. West's Diamond lead gives you some chance because you play last to the trick. If you take dummy's Ace, your Queen will be singleton and you will eventually lose it to the opponents' King. But what if you play a small card from dummy on the first trick, hoping to win with your Queen? If East doesn't have the King, as on the actual hand, your Queen will win the trick and you will no longer have a Diamond loser.

West's choice of opening lead was unfortunate for the defenders, but you had to understand the positional value of playing last to a trick to take advantage of it.

Finessing Against the Queen

Look at this combination of cards:

DUMMY:	♥ A K J
DECLARER:	♥ 6 4 2

You have two sure tricks, the Ace and the King, but you might need to take three tricks in this suit in order to make your contract. Once again, the principle is the same: lead toward the card you hope will take a trick, in this case, the Jack. You are hoping that the opponents' cards look like this:

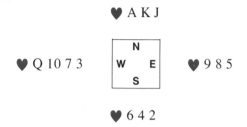

When you lead a small card and West follows with a small card, finesse dummy's Jack. As long as East doesn't have the Queen, you will take three tricks. If East has the Queen, you will take the two tricks you started with. Here is a slight variation of the above combination:

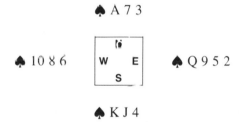

You can play dummy's Ace first, using it as an entry to get to dummy if necessary, and then lead a small card from dummy toward your hand. When East follows with a small card, finesse the Jack, the card you hope will win a trick. As long as West doesn't have the Queen, you will end up with three tricks.

In the above examples, you do not have to lose a trick to the opponents as long as the Queen is favorably placed. When the Jack is in the opposite hand to the Ace and the King, you may have to lose a trick in order to develop the extra trick you need:

DUMMY: ♦ J 7

DECLARER: ♦ A K 5 3

You have two sure tricks, but if you need three, you will have to apply the principle of leading toward the high card, which you hope will win a trick.

Lead a low card from your hand toward the dummy, hoping that the layout of the suit resembles this pattern:

♦ J 7

♦ Q 9 4 2   N W E S   ♦ 10 8 6

♦ A K 5 3

If West plays the Queen, you play dummy's Seven and later, you will take three tricks: the Jack and (assuming there is an entry back to your hand in another suit) the Ace and the King. Notice that you cannot afford to take either the Ace or the King before leading toward dummy's Jack.

You sometimes get opportunities to finesse for cards lower than the Queen. Here is an example in which you might finesse for the Jack:

DUMMY: ♥ A K Q 10 5

DECLARER: ♥ 8 3 2

You would not normally take a finesse with this suit, even though you are missing the Jack. You have eight cards in the suit and the opponents have only five. Usually, the opponents' cards will divide 3-2, so you can play the Ace, King and Queen, and the Ten and Five will be winners. But suppose you play the Ace, on which East follows suit with the Six and West follows suit with the Four. Then you play the King, on which East discards a small Club. Now you know the suit has divided 4-1 and originally looked like this:

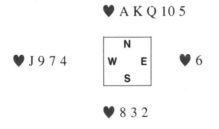

♥ A K Q 10 5

♥ J 9 7 4   N W E S   ♥ 6

♥ 8 3 2

If you carry on and take the Queen, West will take a trick with the Jack. Instead, you must get to your hand with an entry in another suit and lead your remaining small card toward the dummy, then finesse the Ten when West plays a small card.

Let's look at a hand in which you need to finesse for a Queen:

Contract: Four Hearts

West leads ♦K

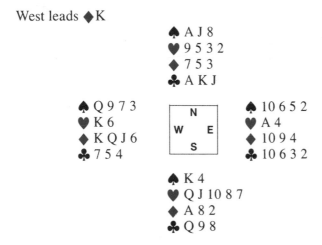

```
                        ♠ A J 8
                        ♥ 9 5 3 2
                        ♦ 7 5 3
                        ♣ A K J

        ♠ Q 9 7 3          N          ♠ 10 6 5 2
        ♥ K 6         W         E     ♥ A 4
        ♦ K Q J 6          S          ♦ 10 9 4
        ♣ 7 5 4                        ♣ 10 6 3 2

                        ♠ K 4
                        ♥ Q J 10 8 7
                        ♦ A 8 2
                        ♣ Q 9 8
```

You can afford three losers. You have two Heart losers, two Diamond losers and no Club or Spade losers. You will definitely lose to the Ace and the King of Hearts, so you must concentrate on trying to eliminate one of your Diamond losers. You can't trump one in dummy and there are no immediate extra tricks on which you can discard one of your losers.

In such a situation, you have to look hard to see if there is any possibility of eliminating your loser. The Jack of Spades in dummy gives you a chance. If West has the Queen, you can take a finesse and create an extra winner in dummy on which you can discard a loser. Let's see how this plan actually works.

Can you afford to draw trump first? No. You will have to let the opponents take the lead when you draw trump, and after you win the first trick with the Ace of Diamonds, you have four quick losers. Win the Ace of Diamonds and play the King of Spades, the high card from the short side. Now lead the four of Spades and, when West follows with a low Spade, finesse dummy's Jack.

Here you will have to hold your breath. If East has the Queen, you will lose a Spade trick you hadn't originally counted on, in addition to the two Heart tricks and two Diamond tricks. You will be defeated in your contract by two tricks. But, if West has the Queen, your Jack will win and you can discard one of your Diamond losers on dummy's Ace of Spades. It is then safe to start drawing the opponents' trump, since you have only three losers left.

Is it worth taking the chance of going down two tricks instead of one while trying to make your contract? Certainly. The penalty for going down one extra trick is much less than the bonus you get for making your game contract. Besides, think of the excitement you'll have waiting to find out which opponent has that missing Queen!

The Finesse as Part of the Plan

Lead toward the high card is a useful piece of advice for developing extra winners in a suit. You can often combine this technique with suit establishment through length. Let's look at an example:

Contract: One No Trump

West leads ♥10

```
                    ♠ 8 7 3
                    ♥ Q 5 2
                    ♦ A Q 4 3 2
                    ♣ 10 3

  ♠ Q 5 2          ┌─────────┐       ♠ K J 9 4
  ♥ 10 9 8 6       │    N    │       ♥ J 7 3
  ♦ K 10 6         │ W     E │       ♦ J 9
  ♣ A 8 4          │    S    │       ♣ K J 7 6
                   └─────────┘
                    ♠ A 10 6
                    ♥ A K 4
                    ♦ 8 7 5
                    ♣ Q 9 5 2
```

You need seven tricks. You have one Spade winner, three Heart winners and one Diamond winner, for a total of five. Two more tricks are needed. The most promising suit is Diamonds: if the finesse works, you can develop one extra trick. However, you will still need another trick to make your contract. You have eight Diamonds and the opponents have five. If the suit breaks 3-2, as you might expect, you can develop two additional Diamond tricks.

To put it all together, you will need an entry to the Diamond winners in dummy once they are established. On this hand, dummy's Queen of Hearts is helpful—provided you do not use it too soon.

Win the first Heart in your hand and play a low Diamond toward the dummy. If West plays low, play the Queen—the card you hope will take a trick—from the dummy. If West plays the King, play the Ace and your Queen will be good on the next round. Either way, your Ace and Queen will win tricks as long as West has the King. You still have to lose a

Diamond trick to the opponents before the suit is established. After taking the Ace and the Queen, play another Diamond. West will win with the King. When you have the lead again, you can go to the dummy with the Queen of Hearts and enjoy the two established Diamond winners to make an overtrick.

As always, when making your plan, you must watch your entries. This is particularly true when you have to take a finesse. On the previous hand, the finesse combined nicely with suit establishment. All you had to do was take your Queen and Ace and give up a Diamond trick. You had an entry in the Heart suit, so that your winners were not stranded. Sometimes you have to exercise more care when you lose your trick to the opponents, since the only entry may be in the suit you are trying to establish.

Contract: Three No Trump

West leads ♥4

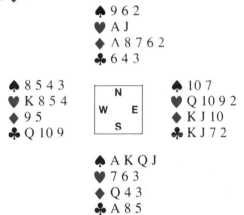

    ♠ 9 6 2
    ♥ A J
    ♦ A 8 7 6 2
    ♣ 6 4 3

♠ 8 5 4 3   ♠ 10 7
♥ K 8 5 4   ♥ Q 10 9 2
♦ 9 5   ♦ K J 10
♣ Q 10 9   ♣ K J 7 2

    ♠ A K Q J
    ♥ 7 6 3
    ♦ Q 4 3
    ♣ A 8 5

You need nine tricks to make the contract. You have four Spades, one Heart, one Diamond and one Club, a total of seven tricks. You need to develop two more tricks. The only hope lies in the Diamond suit. You can plan to take one extra trick by leading toward your Queen. In addition, if the opponents' cards are divided 3-2, you can establish extra tricks through length.

Both conditions exist in the actual hand, but you have to watch your entries when you put it all together. An established suit is of no use unless there is an entry to it. You have both the Ace of Hearts and the Ace of Diamonds in the dummy, the hand with the long Diamonds, so your chances look good. The lead of a Heart, however, uses up your Heart entry before you have an opportunity to establish the Diamonds. Even if you play the Jack on the first trick, East will win with the Queen and play another Heart to make you play your Ace. This means that you will have to be careful to keep the Ace of Diamonds as an entry.

After you win with the Ace of Hearts, take advantage of being in dummy by leading a low Diamond toward the Queen. If East plays the King, you play a small card. The next time you get the lead, you can play the Queen, the high card from the short side, then over to the Ace and, when the suit breaks 3-2, take the other two established Diamond tricks.

If East does not play the King, you must be careful. Play your Queen, which wins the trick. Now you must duck to preserve the entry. Play a small Diamond from your hand and a small Diamond from the dummy, giving up a trick. East will win, but now the Diamonds are established and you have the Ace of Diamonds left as an entry.

Let's look at another example in which you must use your entries carefully.

Contract: Four Hearts

West leads ♠K

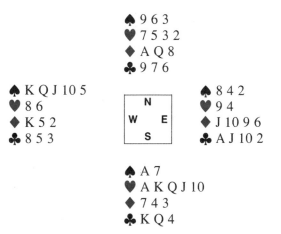

You can afford three losers. You have one Spade loser, two Diamond losers and two Club losers. You have to eliminate two of them. There is no way to eliminate the Spade loser, but both the Diamonds and Clubs offer the possibility of finesses. You hope to take tricks with your Queen of Diamonds and with your King and Queen of Clubs by leading toward your high cards.

After winning the first trick with the Ace of Spades, there is no need to delay drawing trump, because you don't need to trump losers in dummy and you don't have to give up the lead while drawing them. After playing two rounds of trump, you are in your hand, so use the opportunity to play a small Diamond toward the Ace-and-Queen combination in dummy. If West plays a small card, finesse the Queen. You are now in the dummy. Use this entry to play a small Club toward your hand. If East plays a small Club, play your Queen (or King).

Now play another Diamond back to dummy's Ace and repeat the Club finesse by leading a Club toward your hand. If East plays the Ace, your King (or Queen) will win a trick later. If East plays a small card, your King (or Queen) will win the trick. You end up making your contract by carefully using your entries.

Finessing Against More Than One Card

We have looked at cases in which you are concerned with the location of a single missing card. Now let's see what you can do when you are missing two or more key cards. We'll start with this situation:

DUMMY: ♦ A Q 10

DECLARER: ♦ 7 5 3

Without the Ten in dummy, this combination would be equivalent to a straight finesse, assuming that West has the King. However, the Ten gives rise to additional possibilities because you can now consider finessing against the Jack as well as the King. Once again, you should lead toward the high card that you hope will win a trick. The question in this case is, does that description refer to the Ten or to the Queen?

The guideline you can use in these situations is to lead toward the *lower* of your high cards first. Assume you are looking at the suit in isolation in order to take the maximum number of tricks possible from it without being concerned with entries back and forth between the two hands or the possibility of the opponents taking the lead.

Why do you lead toward the lower card first? In the above example, this is the ideal layout:

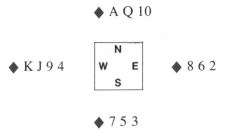

♦ A Q 10

♦ K J 9 4   N W E S   ♦ 8 6 2

♦ 7 5 3

If you play toward the Ten first, West cannot stop you from winning all three tricks.

What would happen if you first played a small card to dummy's Queen, the higher of the two cards? The remaining cards would look like this:

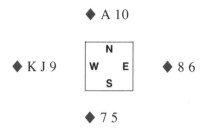

You could come back to your hand and lead toward dummy's Ten, but West would play the Jack (or King) to force you to play dummy's Ace. Then, when you lead the Ten, West will have a higher card left and you will win only two tricks instead of three.

The opponents' cards might originally have been located in this fashion:

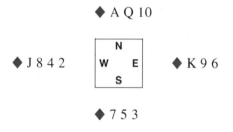

When you play a low card to dummy's Ten, East must play the King to win the trick. You don't have to come back to your hand to repeat the finesse because your Ace and Queen are both established as winners. This is another advantage of playing the Ten the first time.

What if this were the original layout?

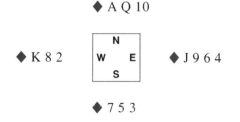

When you play a small card to the Ten, East will win the Jack, and it looks as though you should have played the Queen this time. But nothing is lost. Provided you have an entry back to your hand, you can lead toward the Ace and the Queen in dummy and take a finesse against West's King. You still make two tricks.

Finally, what if this is the case?

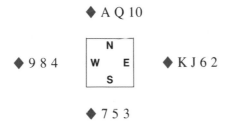

♦ A Q 10

♦ 9 8 4   ♦ K J 6 2

♦ 7 5 3

When you play to dummy's Ten, it loses to East's Jack, and when you get back to your hand and play to dummy's Queen, it loses to East's King. You end up with only one trick. However, there was nothing you could do, since both of the key missing cards were located unfavorably.

In conclusion, leading toward the Ten first does not do any harm, and as you saw in the first layout, you may gain an extra trick.

Now take a look at this combination:

DUMMY: ♥ K J 10
DECLARER: ♥ 8 6 2

You are missing both the Ace and the Queen. Because you have the Ten, you could simply play the King to drive out the opponents' Ace, then play the Jack to drive out their Queen, and end up promoting your Ten as a trick. However, you would like to take two tricks whenever possible and the best chance is by playing from your hand toward dummy, intending to play the Ten (or Jack) first, rather than the King. You are hoping for the following layout:

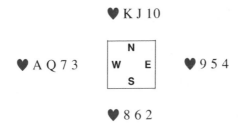

♥ K J 10

♥ A Q 7 3   ♥ 9 5 4

♥ 8 6 2

If West plays a small card, you play your Ten and it wins the trick when East doesn't have a higher card. Now, you can come back to your hand and lead toward dummy again, intending to play the Jack (unless West plays the Queen). West cannot stop you from taking two tricks if you play this way. Notice that if you played the King the first time, you would win one trick, but that would be all. West would have the Ace and Queen left to win both your Jack and Ten.

What if West plays the Ace the first time you lead toward the dummy? Then the remaining cards look like this:

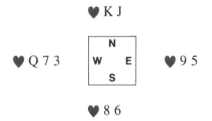

When you regain the lead, you still lead toward dummy and finesse the Jack. Again you end up with two tricks.

Suppose West has the Queen, but East has the Ace?

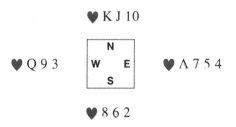

When you play a small card to dummy's Ten (or Jack), East must play the Ace to win the trick. Later you can lead another small card from your hand and repeat the finesse against West's Queen. You still finish with two tricks.

What if East has the Queen and West has the Ace?

When you first play a small card to dummy's Ten, East will win the Queen. You can later drive out West's Ace, but you will only end up with one trick in the suit. However, it would not have helped to lead to dummy's King the first time. You would win the first trick, but the opponents' Queen and Ace would win the next two. Again you would take only one trick.

You would also win only one trick if East had both the Ace and the Queen, but you could not win more by playing the higher card the first time. Once again, you cannot lose by playing to the lower card first in any of the above positions and you can gain a trick whenever West has the Queen.

Let's take a look at a hand in which the principle of leading to the lower of the high cards first helps you make your contract:

Contract: Two Clubs

West leads ♦Q

```
                    ♠ J 7 4 3 2
                    ♥ K 6 3
                    ♦ A 8 7
                    ♣ 6 3

  ♠ A Q 9 6        ┌─────────┐       ♠ 10 8 5
  ♥ J 8 2          │    N    │       ♥ Q 9 7 4
  ♦ Q J 10 6       │ W     E │       ♦ K 9 2
  ♣ 9 8            │    S    │       ♣ A Q 5
                   └─────────┘
                    ♠ K
                    ♥ A 10 5
                    ♦ 5 4 3
                    ♣ K J 10 7 4 2
```

You can afford five losers. You have a Spade loser, a Heart loser, and two Diamond losers, and you are missing both the Ace and the Queen of Clubs. Since there is nothing you can do about the losers in the other suits, you must try to hold your losses in the Club suit to one trick. You will lose one trick to the Ace of Clubs, so you will have to take a finesse against the Queen to make your contract.

After winning a trick with dummy's Ace of Diamonds, you are in the right hand to take a Club finesse by leading toward your high cards. Lead a small Club from dummy and, when East plays a small Club, play the Ten (or Jack), the lower of the cards with which you are hoping to win a trick. Since West does not have the Ace or the Queen, you will win the trick. You now need to get back to the dummy to repeat the finesse. Lead a small Heart to dummy's King and play your remaining small Club toward your hand. If East plays the Ace, you play a small card, then play the King later to draw the last trump. If West plays the Queen, you play the King, which wins the trick. East will get one Club trick, but no more.

Here is a slightly different card combination in which you are missing two key cards:

DUMMY: ◆ A J 10

DECLARER: ◆ 7 6 4

You have one sure trick with dummy's Ace, but it would be nice if you could take a second trick with the Jack or the Ten. When you play a small card from your hand and West follows with a small card, it will do no good to play dummy's Ace since the opponents will still have the King and the Queen left to win the other two tricks in the suit. Once again, play the lower card first, the Ten (or the Jack). There are several ways in which you may get two tricks by following this advice. First, one possible layout of the opponents' cards:

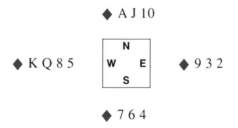

◆ A J 10

◆ K Q 8 5   ◆ 9 3 2

◆ 7 6 4

When you play dummy's Ten, it will win the trick because East does not have a higher card. You still have the Ace left as a second trick. Note that West cannot do any better by playing the Queen (or King) when you lead a small card from your hand. You can win this trick with the Ace and use your Jack (or Ten) to drive out West's remaining high card and promote a second trick in the suit.

You will not always have such a favorable layout of the key missing cards. What happens if East has one of the missing high cards?

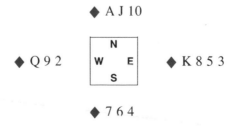

◆ A J 10

◆ Q 9 2   ◆ K 8 5 3

◆ 7 6 4

When you play a small card to dummy's Ten, East wins the trick with the King. However, the remaining cards look like this:

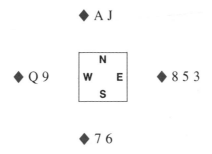

♦ A J

♦ Q 9   N W E S   ♦ 8 5 3

♦ 7 6

When you next take the lead, you can repeat the finesse by playing a small card to dummy's Jack. East cannot win this trick, so once again you end up with two tricks. It would make no difference if West started with the King and East with the Queen. You would lose the first finesse to East's Queen, but win the second finesse against West's King. The only time you will not be successful is when East starts with both the King and the Queen:

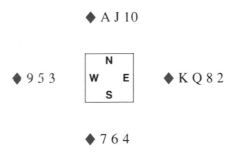

♦ A J 10

♦ 9 5 3   N W E S   ♦ K Q 8 2

♦ 7 6 4

In this case, both of your finesses will lose and you will end up with only one trick. However, with such a very unfavorable position of the opponents' cards, you could not do better by playing the suit differently.

Let's look at one final example. Examine this suit combination:

DUMMY: ♣ Q J 5
DECLARER: ♣ 6 4 2

You are missing both the Ace and the King, so the best you can hope for is one trick from this suit. If you lead the Queen from dummy to drive out the King, then lead the Jack to drive out the Ace, the opponents will still have the Ten left and you won't win a trick. You must use the maxim and start by leading toward the dummy. If West has both the Ace and the King, it will immediately prove fruitful:

♣ Q J 5

```
        N
♣ A K 9 3   W   E   ♣ 10 8 7
        S
```

♣ 6 4 2

If West plays a small card, you will win a trick with dummy's Jack (or Queen) since East does not have a higher card. If West plays the King (or Ace), you will play a small card from dummy and later use dummy's Queen (or Jack) to drive out West's remaining high card, thereby promoting a trick in the suit.

Leading toward the dummy will also prove effective if West has only one of the high cards:

♣ Q J 5

```
        N
♣ K 10 7   W   E   ♣ A 9 8 3
        S
```

♣ 6 4 2

When you play a small card from your hand and West also plays a small card, you play dummy's Jack (or Queen) and East wins the trick with the Ace. The next time you have the opportunity to lead from your hand, you lead another small card toward dummy's Queen. If West plays a small card, dummy's Queen will win the trick immediately, and if West plays the King, dummy's Queen has become a winner for later. Playing the suit in this fashion would also work if West has the Ace and East has the King. The only situation in which you would not take a trick is if East has both the Ace and the King.

We'll finish off with a complete hand in which you have to apply this technique.

Contract: Three No Trump

West leads ♣10

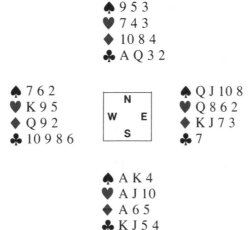

              ♠ 9 5 3
              ♥ 7 4 3
              ♦ 10 8 4
              ♣ A Q 3 2

♠ 7 6 2   ♠ Q J 10 8
♥ K 9 5   ♥ Q 8 6 2
♦ Q 9 2   ♦ K J 7 3
♣ 10 9 8 6   ♣ 7

              ♠ A K 4
              ♥ A J 10
              ♦ A 6 5
              ♣ K J 5 4

You need nine tricks; you have two Spades, one Heart, one Diamond and four Clubs, for a total of eight. You need to develop one more trick. Your only chance is in the Heart suit. You can hope to take a trick with either your Ten or your Jack in addition to the Ace.

Win the first Club in the dummy. Lead a small Heart toward your hand and, when East plays a small card, play the Ten (or the Jack). West wins the trick with the King. Whatever he returns, you win, and go back over to the dummy with your remaining Club entry and again lead a small Heart toward your hand. When East plays a small card, finesse the Jack. This time, the finesse works and you take the extra trick you need to make your contract.

Summary

The finesse is one of the most useful techniques that you can use to develop extra winners. It is an attempt to win a trick with a card that is lower-ranking than one of those held by the opponents and its success depends on a favorable position of particular cards in the opponents' hands. The general principle can be remembered by the following advice:

KEY MAXIM

Lead Toward the High Card

This maxim reminds you to lead toward the card you hope will take the trick. If you are finessing for more than one card, lead toward the lower of your high cards first, repeating the finesse if necessary.

Exercises

1) You are in a contract of Three No Trump. How do you plan to make nine tricks?

♠ A Q J 3
♥ 8 6 4
♦ K 7 6
♣ 9 7 6

West leads ♦J

```
      N
  W       E
      S
```

♠ 7 6 5
♥ A K 2
♦ A Q 4
♣ A 8 4 3

Solution

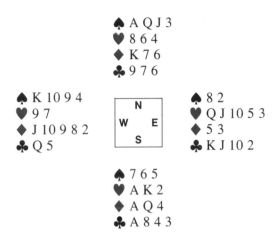

You need nine tricks. You have one sure trick in Spades, two in Hearts, three in Diamonds and one in Clubs: you need two more. Since you have seven Clubs, you might be able to establish one trick in the Club suit if the opponents' cards break 3-3. However, the Spade suit represents a better possibility. You can hope that West has the King and try a finesse, repeating it if necessary. Even if East has the King, there is still the possibility that the opponents' cards will divide 3-3 and you will get three tricks in the suit anyway.

Win the first Diamond trick in your hand, because you want to lead toward dummy. Play a small Spade and when West follows with a small card, play dummy's Jack (or Queen). When you win the trick, come back to your hand with either a Diamond or a Heart winner and lead another small Spade toward the dummy. When West plays a small card, repeat the finesse by playing dummy's Queen. You win and you have the nine tricks you need. You can play dummy's Ace to see if the Spade suit breaks 3-3 and you make an overtrick. On this hand, the Spades are 4-2, so you will have to settle for nine tricks.

2) Once again you are in Three No Trump. Where will your nine tricks come from?

♠ A 8 7 3
♥ Q 3
♦ A 8 2
♣ J 10 6 4

West leads ♠2

```
    N
W       E
    S
```

♠ K 6
♥ A 9 6 2
♦ 10 7 5
♣ A K Q 3

Solution

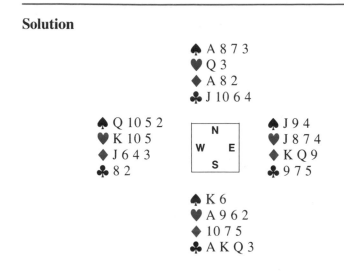

♠ A 8 7 3
♥ Q 3
♦ A 8 2
♣ J 10 6 4

♠ Q 10 5 2
♥ K 10 5
♦ J 6 4 3
♣ 8 2

♠ J 9 4
♥ J 8 7 4
♦ K Q 9
♣ 9 7 5

♠ K 6
♥ A 9 6 2
♦ 10 7 5
♣ A K Q 3

You need nine tricks and start with eight: two Spades, one Heart, one Diamond and four Clubs. Your only hope for an extra trick is in the Heart suit. Dummy has the Queen and you hope that West has the King.

Win the first trick in your hand with the King of Spades, then lead a small Heart toward the dummy. You cannot afford to play the Ace first. If West plays a small Heart, play dummy's Queen and hope that East does not have the King. If West plays the King, play a small card from dummy and your Queen will be a trick later on. When the finesse works, you have nine tricks.

3) This time you are in Four Hearts. How do you plan to make one of your losers disappear?

♠ Q J 8
♥ K J 9 6
♦ A 8 2
♣ K 7 5

West leads ♦ J

	N	
W		E
	S	

♠ 9 3
♥ A Q 10 8 5
♦ K 6 3
♣ A 10 8

Solution

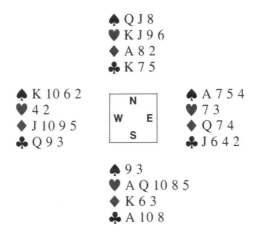

♠ Q J 8
♥ K J 9 6
♦ A 8 2
♣ K 7 5

♠ K 10 6 2
♥ 4 2
♦ J 10 9 5
♣ Q 9 3

♠ A 7 5 4
♥ 7 3
♦ Q 7 4
♣ J 6 4 2

♠ 9 3
♥ A Q 10 8 5
♦ K 6 3
♣ A 10 8

You can afford three losers. You have two Spade losers, one Diamond loser and one Club loser . . . one loser too many. You can't trump any of your losers in the dummy, so you look for somewhere to discard one. There is no immediate extra winner in dummy, but if you lead toward the high card, you might be able to develop an extra winner in the Spade suit.

Can you afford to draw trump first? On this hand, yes, you can. You can draw trump without losing a trick and you do not need your trump for other purposes. Win the opening lead with dummy's Ace of Diamonds, because you want to preserve entries to your hand, so that you can lead toward dummy's Spades. Draw trump by playing a Heart to the King and a Heart back to your Ace. When the missing trump divides 2-2, you don't have to draw any more and you are in your hand, so you can lead a Spade toward dummy. When West plays a small card, play dummy's Jack (or Queen). It will lose to East's Ace. Suppose East leads a Diamond. You can win this trick in your hand with the King and lead your remaining small Spade toward dummy. If West doesn't play the King, you will play dummy's Queen, which will win the trick. You will not lose two Spade tricks. If West does win the King of Spades, dummy's Queen is now established as an extra winner. The opponents can take a Diamond trick, but that will be your last loser. Whatever they lead now, you can win and play a Club to dummy's King, then discard your Club loser on the Queen of Spades.

10

Lead Toward the High Card . . . The Other Side of the Coin

In the previous chapter, we saw that one of the common ways to develop extra tricks is to lead toward the high card that you hope will take a trick. It is a very effective play, but in this chapter we will see that there are times when declarer should not lead toward the high card.

To decide when to lead a high card rather than lead toward it, you must examine the cards you hold in the suit to see if you can afford to lead a high card—and you must keep in mind your overall plan for making your contract.

In the previous chapter, we looked at the following combination:

DUMMY: ♥ A 8 4

DECLARER: ♥ Q 7 2

With one sure trick, the Ace, you hope to get a second trick by leading toward your Queen. You are hoping that East has the King and the opponents' cards look something like this:

♥ A 8 4

♥ 10 6 5   N W E S   ♥ K J 9 3

♥ Q 7 2

As long as East has the King, you can always end up with two tricks by leading toward the Queen. Notice that it doesn't do any good to lead the

Queen from your hand. If East has the King, as in the above example, the Queen will be taken by the King and you will take only one trick in the suit, the Ace, because the opponents have the remaining high cards. Similarly, it does you no good to lead the Queen first if West has the King:

♥ A 8 4

♥ K J 9 3   ♥ 6 5 2

♥ Q 7 2

If you lead the Queen, West will **cover** (play a higher card) with the King, making you play dummy's Ace to win the trick. The opponents will have the Jack and the Ten left to win the next two tricks in the suit.

In the above situation, you had to be careful to lead toward the Queen because you were missing the Jack and the Ten. You could not afford to lead the high card, the Queen, because if one of the opponents played the King on it (covered with the King), they would end up promoting tricks for their side instead of for your side.

When You Can Afford to Lead a High Card

If you hold the Jack and the Ten, the situation is a little different.

DUMMY: ♥ A 8 4

DECLARER: ♥ Q J 10

The combined holding in the suit is much stronger, because you are only missing the King. With this holding, you can always obtain two tricks by force. You can take the Ace and lead the Queen, or lead toward the Queen, and drive out the King. Whether East or West has the King, you will promote the Jack as a second trick. However, with a holding so strong, you can do even better if West has the King:

♥ A 8 4

♥ K 9 7 3   ♥ 6 5 2

♥ Q J 10

You can lead the Queen (or Jack or Ten) from your hand first! If West covers with the King, you win the trick with dummy's Ace and have the Jack and Ten left as tricks. If West does not cover with the King, you can play a small card from the dummy and your Queen will win the trick, because East does not have the King. You can then lead the Jack and, again, West's King is trapped. If he plays a small card, you play a small card from dummy and win the trick. If West covers the Jack, you win with dummy's Ace and your Ten is promoted into a winner. You will win three tricks no matter what West does. Of course, if East has the King, your finesse will lose and East will win a trick. However, you will still make two tricks and are no worse off for having tried to trap West's King.

Since you were missing the King in both this example and the previous example, how can you tell when to lead a high card and when to lead *toward* a high card? The answer is to look at the other cards you have in the suit. You can lead a high card *if you can afford to have the opponents cover it with a higher card.* In the above example, you could afford to lead the Queen, because if West put the King on it, your Jack and Ten would be promoted to winners. We can contrast this situation with the earlier example:

DUMMY: ♥ A 8 4

DECLARER: ♥ Q 7 2

In this case, you cannot afford to lead the Queen, because if West covers it with the King, it is the opponents' Jack and Ten that will be promoted into winners. Instead, you must lead *toward* the Queen if you hope to take a trick with it.

The high cards can be distributed in various ways between the two hands and the principle still applies:

DUMMY: ♦ A J 5

DECLARER: ♦ Q 10 3

Here you can again afford to lead the Queen (or Ten) from your hand. If West covers with the King, the Jack and Ten will be promoted into winners and you will take all three tricks. If East ends up winning the first trick with the King, you will still have the Ace and the Jack left for two tricks in the suit and could have done no better by playing the cards in any other fashion.

Here is an opportunity to trap the opponents' Queen:

DUMMY: ♠ J 10 3

DECLARER: ♠ A K 5

You can always take two tricks merely by playing the Ace and the King. However, if you play in this manner, you will not get three tricks unless one of the opponents has a singleton or doubleton Queen, which is quite unlikely. To try for three tricks, lead the Jack from dummy and hope that the opponents' cards are distributed in this manner:

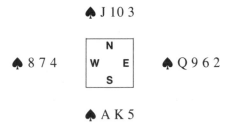

♠ J 10 3

♠ 8 7 4   ♠ Q 9 6 2

♠ A K 5

When you lead the Jack, it will do East no good to cover with the Queen. You will win with the Ace (or the King) and the Ten will be promoted into a trick. If East does not cover the Jack, you play the Five from your hand and the Jack wins the trick since West does not have a higher card. You still have the Ace and King left for three tricks in the suit. If it turns out that West has the Queen, you are back to the two tricks you started with.

Let's see how leading a high card to trap an opponent's high card can be useful in a complete hand:

Contract: Three No Trump

West leads ♠ 10

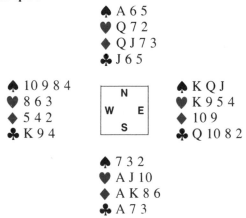

♠ A 6 5
♥ Q 7 2
♦ Q J 7 3
♣ J 6 5

♠ 10 9 8 4   ♠ K Q J
♥ 8 6 3   ♥ K 9 5 4
♦ 5 4 2   ♦ 10 9
♣ K 9 4   ♣ Q 10 8 2

♠ 7 3 2
♥ A J 10
♦ A K 8 6
♣ A 7 3

You need nine tricks and start with seven: one Spade, one Heart, four Diamonds and one Club. The best prospects for extra tricks are in the Heart suit. You are only missing the King, and if you can trap it, you will end up with the two extra tricks you need.

After you win dummy's Ace of Spades, you can afford to lead the Queen of Hearts. If East plays the King, you will win the trick with your Ace, and your Jack and Ten will be winners. If East plays a small card, play the Ten from your hand and Dummy's Queen will win the trick, because West doesn't have the King. Then lead a small card from dummy toward the remaining Ace and Jack in your hand and whatever East does, you will end up taking three Heart tricks and making your contract. You could afford to lead dummy's Queen of Hearts because it didn't matter whether or not East covered with the King.

Determining whether or not you can afford to have the opponents cover your high card sometimes requires a bit of thought. Take a look at this combination:

DUMMY: ♦ A Q 6

DECLARER: ♦ J 5 2

You have one sure trick and can always promote a second trick using the Queen to drive out the opponents' King, establishing the Jack as a winner. But what if you need to take three tricks? Can you afford to lead the Jack? You must ask yourself what will happen if West covers with the King. You will have to win the trick with dummy's Ace. You can take a second trick with the Queen, but since the opponents have the Ten, you will not get a third trick.

This tells you not to lead the Jack. What should you do? This is not the time to lead toward the Jack, because one of the opponents will win with the King and you will again end up with exactly two tricks. Your only hope is to lead a small card, not the Jack, from your hand toward the dummy, planning to finesse dummy's Queen if West plays a small card. You will have to hope that the opponents' cards are distributed like this:

♦ A Q 6

♦ K 9
```
┌───────┐
│   N   │
│ W   E │
│   S   │
└───────┘
```
♦ 10 8 7 4 3

♦ J 5 2

You play a small card to dummy's Queen and then play the Ace. West has to play the King when you play the Ace and now you can lead dummy's Six to your Jack, ending up with three tricks. You would be lucky to find the cards distributed in this manner, but by knowing that you couldn't afford to lead the Jack, you would be able to take advantage of the favorable position.

Here is another example in which you must be careful:

DUMMY: ♣ J 7 5 3

DECLARER: ♣ A K 6 2

In the previous chapter, we saw a similar combination and ended up leading toward the Jack, hoping that West had the Queen. That strategy is fine if you can afford to lose a trick in the suit, but what if you can't? Should you plan to lead dummy's Jack and take a finesse if East plays a small card? Once again, you must ask yourself if you can afford to have the Jack covered by the Queen. If you lead the Jack and East covers it with the Queen, you will be forced to win with the Ace (or the King). You can take your remaining high card, but since you will only have small cards left, the opponents will have a winner in the suit even if it breaks 3-2.

What is your alternative? You can take the Ace and the King and hope that one of the opponents has a **doubleton** Queen. You will then be able to win the third trick with your Jack and, when the suit breaks 3-2, end up with no losers in the suit. For example, the suit might be distributed like this:

♣ J 7 5 3

♣ 10 9 4
<table>
<tr><td></td><td>N</td><td></td></tr>
<tr><td>W</td><td></td><td>E</td></tr>
<tr><td></td><td>S</td><td></td></tr>
</table>
♣ Q 8

♣ A K 6 2

Examine the layout carefully to see what happens if you lead the Jack from dummy, instead of a small card, and East covers with the Queen. Knowing the principle that you only lead a high card if you can afford to have it covered by the opponents will help whenever you are faced with an unfamiliar combination of cards in a suit.

Watching Your Entries

If a finesse may have to be repeated, you must be careful to ensure that there are sufficient entries to allow you to do it. A common way to preserve entries is to lead a high card when you can afford it. Look at this example:

DUMMY: ♥ 10 9 3

DECLARER: ♥ A Q J 8 5

With these cards, you would like to trap East's King. The general principle, as we saw in the last chapter, is to lead a small card from dummy toward your hand and, when East plays a small card, finesse the Jack (or the Queen). If it works, you will go back to dummy and repeat the finesse, but only if you have an entry to dummy in another suit. Sometimes you do not have the luxury of additional entries to the dummy. In such cases, you start off by leading a high card from the dummy, the Ten (or the Nine) in the above example. Let's see why this strategy works:

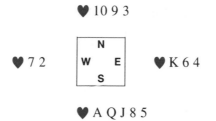

♥ 10 9 3

♥ 7 2   ♥ K 6 4

♥ A Q J 8 5

If East covers with the King when you lead the Ten, you can win with the Ace and you have the rest of the tricks in the suit. If East does not cover the Ten, you play a small card from your hand and the Ten wins the trick. You are still in the dummy and can repeat the finesse by leading the Nine. Whatever East plays, you cannot be prevented from taking all the tricks in the suit.

This is a similar example:

DUMMY: ♠ A Q 10

DECLARER: ♠ J 6 3

You are intending to take a finesse against West's King. Holding the Ten, you can afford to lead the Jack from your hand because if West covers with the King, you will have all the high cards. If West doesn't cover with the King, play the Ten from dummy and you will still be in your hand to repeat the finesse.

Here is a final example:

DUMMY: ♦ Q 4 3

DECLARER: ♦ A J 10

If you are short of entries in the dummy, play the Queen first. If East covers with the King, you will take three tricks in the suit. If East doesn't cover, and your Queen wins the trick, you are in the right place to repeat the finesse.

Here is an example from a complete hand:

Contract: Three Spades

West leads ♣K

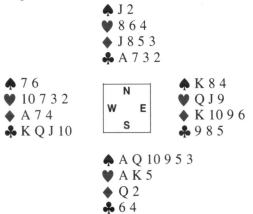

                    ♠ J 2
                    ♥ 8 6 4
                    ♦ J 8 5 3
                    ♣ A 7 3 2

♠ 7 6   ♠ K 8 4
♥ 10 7 3 2   ♥ Q J 9
♦ A 7 4   ♦ K 10 9 6
♣ K Q J 10   ♣ 9 8 5

                    ♠ A Q 10 9 5 3
                    ♥ A K 5
                    ♦ Q 2
                    ♣ 6 4

You can afford four losers. You are missing the King of Spades for one potential loser and have one loser in Hearts, two in Diamonds and one in Clubs. You plan to eliminate your Spade loser by taking a finesse against the King, assuming that East has it.

However, you must be careful. You only have one entry to dummy, the Ace of Clubs, and you will need to repeat the Spade finesse if East does not have a singleton or doubleton King. After winning the Ace of Clubs, lead the Jack of Spades from dummy. If East covers with the King, play the Ace and draw the rest of the opponents' trump. If East plays a small card, play a small card from your hand. When the Jack wins the trick, you are still in the dummy and can repeat the finesse.

Safety First

There are often times when you can take a trick with one of your high cards first, before taking a finesse. Look at this suit:

DUMMY: ♦ A K J

DECLARER: ♦ 7 5 3

To take three tricks in this suit, you plan to play a small card from your hand and finesse dummy's Jack, hoping that West has the Queen. However, provided that you have sufficient entries to your hand, it does no harm to first take dummy's Ace (or King) and then come to your hand to play a small card toward dummy. This prevents the loss of a trick when the actual layout of the cards is as follows:

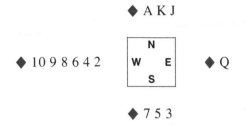

◆ A K J

◆ 10 9 8 6 4 2

◆ Q

◆ 7 5 3

By playing the Ace first, you will find out that East started with a singleton Queen and you don't need to finesse. The above distribution is unlikely, but it doesn't hurt to play it safe whenever possible. Here is a similar situation:

DUMMY: ♣ Q 8 5 2

DECLARER: ♣ A 6 4 3

You plan to lead a small card toward dummy's Queen, hoping that West has the King. However, it does no harm to take the Ace first, in case this is the complete layout:

♣ Q 8 5 2

♣ J 10 9 7

♣ K

♣ A 6 4 3

In general, you should play one or more of your high cards first whenever you can afford it. However, the question of whether or not you can afford it is sometimes tricky. Look at this suit:

DUMMY: ♥ 6 5

DECLARER: ♥ A K J 10

If you want to take all four tricks, you have to hope that East has the Queen. It may seem that you can afford to take a trick with the Ace (or the King) first, in case West has a singleton Queen. But that would leave only one small card in dummy. You could take one finesse against East's Queen, but you could not repeat it. You would now have to hope that East started with only two or three cards in the suit. If East has four or more cards, including the Queen, you will end up with only three tricks in the suit. By taking a high card first to guard against West having a singleton

Queen, you lose a trick whenever West started with any other singleton or doubleton or three small cards.

Here is an example of a complete hand in which it pays off to play a high card first:

Contract: Four Spades

West leads ♥K

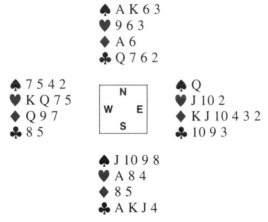

♠ A K 6 3
♥ 9 6 3
♦ A 6
♣ Q 7 6 2

♠ 7 5 4 2
♥ K Q 7 5
♦ Q 9 7
♣ 8 5

♠ Q
♥ J 10 2
♦ K J 10 4 3 2
♣ 10 9 3

♠ J 10 9 8
♥ A 8 4
♦ 8 5
♣ A K J 4

You can afford three losers. You are missing the Queen of Spades and you have two Heart losers and a Diamond loser. You cannot do anything about the losers in Hearts and Diamonds, so you must avoid losing a trick to the Queen of Spades. You plan to do this by taking a finesse against West's Queen.

You can afford to lead the Jack from your hand since, if West covers with the Queen, you have the remaining high cards. However, you don't need both the Ace and the King in dummy to trap West's Queen . . . you can afford to play one of your high cards first. On this hand, the extra caution is rewarded when it turns out that East started with the singleton Queen. You no longer need the finesse and can draw trump and then take your winners to make the contract.

When You Can't Afford to Lead Toward the High Card

Always keep the objective in mind when playing the hand. There are often situations when you would like to lead toward the high card in a particular suit, but your plan reveals that you can't because there isn't a suitable entry to the other hand or you don't have the time to do what you would like.

Here is an example in a complete hand:

Contract: Three No Trump

West leads: ♦Q

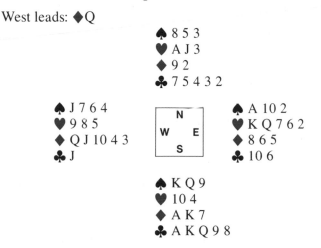

```
                    ♠ 8 5 3
                    ♥ A J 3
                    ♦ 9 2
                    ♣ 7 5 4 3 2
  ♠ J 7 6 4                        ♠ A 10 2
  ♥ 9 8 5          N               ♥ K Q 7 6 2
  ♦ Q J 10 4 3    W   E            ♦ 8 6 5
  ♣ J              S               ♣ 10 6
                    ♠ K Q 9
                    ♥ 10 4
                    ♦ A K 7
                    ♣ A K Q 9 8
```

You need nine tricks. You have one sure trick in Hearts, two in Diamonds and five in Clubs. You need only one more. The Spade suit can provide it because you can use the King to drive out the opponents' Ace and promote the Queen into a winner.

Considering the Spade suit by itself, you may be tempted to lead toward your King and Queen in case East has the Ace. By doing that, you might end up with two tricks in the suit. But there are a number of reasons why it is not a good idea on this particular hand.

First, you don't need two tricks from the Spade suit to make your contract, only one. Second, you need an entry to get to dummy to lead toward your hand. The only sure entry is the Ace of Hearts. If you play a Heart to dummy's Ace before leading Spades, you put the contract in jeopardy. When the opponents win a trick with the Ace of Spades, they will be able to take their Heart tricks since you no longer have any way to stop them. In the actual hand, East can take the Ace of Spades and four Heart tricks once your Ace is gone, thereby defeating the contract. Finally, one entry to dummy is not really enough. To get two tricks in Spades you are going to have to lead twice toward your King and Queen if East plays a small card the first time.

All things considered, keep it simple by winning the first Diamond trick and leading your King (or Queen) of Spades to develop the extra trick you need. From there on, it's clear sailing.

Here is an interesting card combination:

DUMMY: ♥ A 5 2

DECLARER: ♥ Q J 4

This situation is similar to an earlier example, but this time, you don't have the Ten. You can take two tricks by playing the Ace and then leading the Queen (or Jack) to drive out the opponents' King and promote your remaining high card. This has the same effect as leading toward your Queen (or Jack).

What if you lead the Queen (or Jack) from your hand? If East has the King, your finesse will lose and you will end up with the same two tricks. If West has the King, the Queen will be covered by it, forcing you to play the Ace to win the trick. You have a second trick with the Jack, but once again, you cannot take any more tricks because the opponents have the Ten.

It would seem that there is no advantage to leading the Queen from your hand, but if West has the King, you can take two tricks *without losing the lead to the opponents*. It might prove useful when making your plan:

Contract: One No Trump

West leads: ♣K

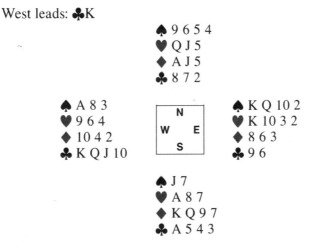

You need seven winners and start with one Heart, four Diamonds and one Club. Your extra trick can be developed in the Heart suit by using the Queen to drive out the opponents' King, thereby promoting your Jack to a winner.

But, in making your plan, you must watch the opponents. If you let them take the lead with the King of Hearts, they are in a position to take all their

Club and Spade winners, of which they have more than enough to defeat the contract. You must establish your extra Heart winner without giving up the lead. This can be done if East has the King. When you win the Club Ace, play a Diamond to dummy's Ace so that you can lead the Queen of Hearts from dummy. If East covers with the King, win with the Ace—now dummy's Jack will be the seventh trick. If East plays a small card, play a small card from your hand. When the finesse wins, you again have seven winners, so take your tricks and run.

One more example:

Contract: Three Spades

West leads: ♣K

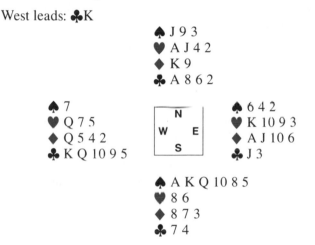

♠ J 9 3
♥ A J 4 2
♦ K 9
♣ A 8 6 2

♠ 7
♥ Q 7 5
♦ Q 5 4 2
♣ K Q 10 9 5

♠ 6 4 2
♥ K 10 9 3
♦ A J 10 6
♣ J 3

♠ A K Q 10 8 5
♥ 8 6
♦ 8 7 3
♣ 7 4

You can afford four losers. You have one Heart loser, three Diamond losers and a Club loser. To eliminate one of the Diamond losers you might try leading toward dummy's King, hoping that West has the Ace. Another possibility is to plan to trump one of your Diamond losers in the dummy.

Can you afford to do both? If you want to lead a Diamond toward dummy's King, you must first get to your hand. The only entries are in the trump suit. Suppose you win the first trick with dummy's Ace of Clubs and play a Spade to the Ace. Next you lead a Diamond toward dummy's King, but unfortunately, East wins with the Ace. What if East leads another Spade? Now you only have one trump left in dummy. When you give up a second Diamond trick, East can win and lead Spades again. You will no longer have any trump left in dummy with which to trump the Diamond loser.

There is no time to try leading a Diamond toward dummy. Instead, win the first trick and immediately lead a Diamond from the dummy, either the King or the Nine. East can win and lead a trump, but you win the trick, then lead another Diamond. East wins and tries leading another trump, but you can win this trick in your hand, lead your remaining Diamond and trump it in dummy. You win the race—*if* you don't take time out to lead toward your high card.

The best play for an individual suit may not be the best play for the entire hand. Always make a complete plan before deciding how to play a particular suit.

More on Finesses

We'll finish off this chapter with two more situations in which you must decide whether or not to lead the high card.

In the previous chapter, we looked at this card combination:

DUMMY: ♦ A J 10

DECLARER: ♦ 7 6 4

The best chance for two tricks in this suit is to start off by leading a small card toward dummy and to play the Ten (or Jack) if West plays a small card. If East wins the first trick with the King or the Queen, you later repeat the finesse by leading a small card toward dummy's remaining Ace and Jack. The second finesse will work if West started with one of the two missing high cards, the King or the Queen, and you end up with two tricks. Only if East has both the King and the Queen, so that both your finesses fail, will you take only one trick.

Now look at this combination:

DUMMY: ♣ A 6 4

DECLARER: ♣ J 10 9

This situation is similar to that in the previous example, except that instead of leading toward the card you hope will win a trick, the Jack or the Ten, you will have to lead them from your hand and try to trap the King or the Queen in West's hand. Let's see how this plan works when West holds the King:

                                ♣ A 6 4

                        ┌─────────┐
    ♣ K 8 3 2   │   N   │   ♣ Q 7 5
                        │ W   E │
                        │   S   │
                        └─────────┘

                                ♣ J 10 9

If West plays the King when you lead the Jack from your hand, you can win the trick with dummy's Ace, then use your Ten to drive out East's Queen and establish the Nine as a second trick. If West plays a small card when the Jack is led, play a small card from the dummy and lose the first trick to East's Queen. The remaining cards look like this:

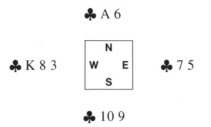

When you regain the lead, play the Ten (or the Nine) from your hand. If West covers, your remaining card is promoted into a winner. If West plays a small card, play a small card from dummy and this time your finesse will succeed. Notice how important the Nine is. With the Nine, you can lead a high card from your hand because you can afford to have the opponent cover it, and eventually your Nine is promoted to a trick.

In the above example, you would also take two tricks if West started with the Queen and East started with the King, or if West started with both the King and the Queen. The only time you would not make two tricks is when East has both the King and the Queen.

The following is a combination of cards in which you are missing the Queen and have a choice as to which opponent you hope has the missing card:

DUMMY: ♠ A J 3

DECLARER: ♠ K 10 4

If you hope that West has the missing Queen, win the first trick with the King in your hand and lead one of your remaining cards toward dummy's Ace and Jack. If West plays a small card, finesse dummy's Jack and hope that East can't win the trick with the Queen. If you suspect that East has the Queen, win the first trick with dummy's Ace and play dummy's Three (or Jack) toward the King and Ten remaining in your hand. If East plays a small card, play the Ten and hope that West didn't start with the Queen.

A position such as this is called a **two-way finesse** because you have the option of taking the finesse either way. How do you know which opponent has the missing Queen? On many hands it is a pure guess ... you pay your money and you take your chances. However, sometimes the bidding by the opponents provides a clue. You might expect that an opponent who has opened the bidding or made an overcall is more likely to be holding the missing Queen.

Here is another combination of cards that requires some thought:

> DUMMY: ♥ K 7 6 3
>
> DECLARER: ♥ Q 5 4 2

You can always obtain one trick from this holding by leading the King (or the Queen) to drive out the opponents' Ace, thereby promoting your remaining high card as a winner. In addition, you have eight cards and the opponents have five, so if the opponents' cards break 3-2, you can establish a second trick through length.

However, you may need to take three tricks from this suit. As usual, you should start off by leading toward one of your high cards rather than just leading it.

Which high card should you lead toward? That depends on which opponent you think has the Ace. Suppose you suspect that West has the Ace. Lead a small card from your hand toward dummy. If West plays the Ace, play a small card from dummy and later your King and Queen will both take tricks. But what if West plays a small card and you play dummy's King, which wins the trick? Now the remaining cards are:

> DUMMY: ♥ 7 6 3
>
> DECLARER: ♥ Q 5 4

Normally, you lead toward the high card you hope will win a trick, but that plan won't work in this case. When you lead a small card from dummy and East plays a small card, you know that it will do no good to play the Queen because West has the Ace. Instead, you must play a small card from your hand as well and hope that the original layout looked like this:

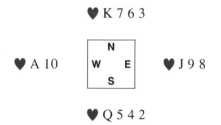

> ♥ K 7 6 3
>
> ♥ A 10   ♥ J 9 8
>
> ♥ Q 5 4 2

After you have played a small card to dummy's King, West has only the Ace left, so you don't need to waste the Queen on the second trick. Play a small card and you will end up with three tricks in the suit: the King, the Queen and your remaining small card.

As mentioned earlier, you could also start by leading a small card toward your Queen if you think East has the Ace. You will also have to hope that East has only two cards in the suit. Your decision to play West for the Ace or East for the Ace is based on a guess, but you might be influenced by the bidding when making your decision.

Summary

While the maxim lead toward your high card is a very valuable piece of advice, it should not be used blindly. There are times when you can afford to lead a high card rather than lead toward it. The most common situations in which you lead a high card are:

- When you can afford to have the opponents cover it with a higher card
- When you can afford to lead one high card before leading toward another
- When you do not have, or cannot afford, entries to the other hand.

Exercises

1) You reach a contract of Three No Trump. How do you plan to make it?

♠ Q J 10
♥ J 7 3
♦ A 6 5
♣ Q 9 6 4

West leads ♦7

```
    N
W       E
    S
```

♠ A 6 4
♥ A 5 2
♦ 9 3 2
♣ A K J 5

Solution

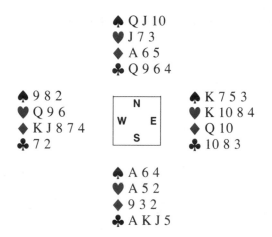

♠ Q J 10
♥ J 7 3
♦ A 6 5
♣ Q 9 6 4

♠ 9 8 2
♥ Q 9 6
♦ K J 8 7 4
♣ 7 2

♠ K 7 5 3
♥ K 10 8 4
♦ Q 10
♣ 10 8 3

♠ A 6 4
♥ A 5 2
♦ 9 3 2
♣ A K J 5

You need nine winners and start with seven: one Spade, one Heart, one Diamond and four Clubs. The two extra winners can come from the Spade suit *if* you can trap East's King.

After winning the Diamond trick with dummy's Ace, lead the Queen (or the Jack or the Ten) of Spades from dummy. You can lead the high card because if East covers with the King, the Jack and the Ten will be promoted into the two extra winners you need. If East doesn't cover with the King, play a small card from your hand. When West can't win the trick, continue by leading another high card from dummy and repeating the finesse. As long as East has the King, you wind up with the nine winners you need to make the contract.

2) You are in a contract of Four Spades. How do you plan to play the contract to give yourself the best chance of making it?

♠ 10 4 3
♥ A 8 7 3
♦ 6 5 2
♣ Q 7 4

West leads ♣10

```
      N
 W        E
      S
```

♠ A Q J 8 7 2
♥ K 2
♦ A 8 7
♣ A 2

Solution

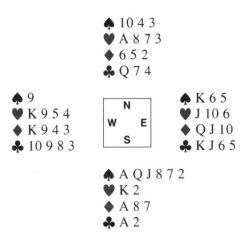

```
              ♠ 10 4 3
              ♥ A 8 7 3
              ♦ 6 5 2
              ♣ Q 7 4
♠ 9                          ♠ K 6 5
♥ K 9 5 4      N             ♥ J 10 6
♦ K 9 4 3   W     E          ♦ Q J 10
♣ 10 9 8 3     S             ♣ K J 6 5
              ♠ A Q J 8 7 2
              ♥ K 2
              ♦ A 8 7
              ♣ A 2
```

You can afford three losers. You have one in Spades, two in Diamonds and one in Clubs. You have to eliminate one loser. There are two possibilities. You can hope that West has the King of Clubs and that dummy's Queen will win a trick. You can also hope that East has the King of Spades and that you can trap it by taking a finesse.

How do you put it all together? Since West has led a Club, you can try the Club finesse by playing dummy's Queen. If West started with the King, dummy's Queen will win and you will have eliminated one of your losers. Unfortunately, on the actual hand, East has the King and covers your Queen with it. You will have to rely on the Spade finesse.

Be careful: dummy has only one entry, the Ace of Hearts. After winning the Ace of Clubs, play a small Heart to dummy's Ace and lead the Ten of Spades. You can afford to lead the Ten because if East covers, you have the remaining high cards. If East doesn't cover, play a low Spade from your hand. When the finesse works, you are still in dummy and can repeat it.

3) With your powerful hand, you end up in a contract of Three No Trump. Can you afford to take the Heart finesse to make your contract?

♠ 8 6 4
♥ 8 7 5 2
♦ A 8
♣ 10 8 4 2

West leads ♠Q

```
    N
W       E
    S
```

♠ A K 3
♥ A Q J
♦ 10 3 2
♣ A K Q J

Solution

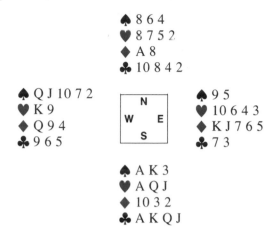

♠ 8 6 4
♥ 8 7 5 2
♦ A 8
♣ 10 8 4 2

♠ Q J 10 7 2
♥ K 9
♦ Q 9 4
♣ 9 6 5

♠ 9 5
♥ 10 6 4 3
♦ K J 7 6 5
♣ 7 3

♠ A K 3
♥ A Q J
♦ 10 3 2
♣ A K Q J

You need nine tricks and start with eight: two Spades, one Heart, one Diamond and four Clubs. The extra winner can be developed in the Heart suit. Ideally, you would like to lead a Heart from dummy toward the high cards in your hand, and plan to take a finesse against East's King.

Can you afford to do this? The only entry to dummy is the Ace of Diamonds. If you play a Diamond to the Ace and lead a Heart to your Jack (or Queen), you will be in trouble if it loses. The opponents' Diamonds will be established, and if they can take four tricks, in addition to the Heart trick, your contract will be defeated.

Instead, you can play it safe. You need only one extra trick and you can take it by playing the Ace of Hearts and then the Queen to drive out the opponents' King, thereby promoting your Jack into a winner. There is no need to risk your contract by taking a Heart finesse.

11

Eight Ever, Nine Never

In the earlier chapters, you saw that one method of developing extra tricks is through length. For example, if you have the following suit, you hope to take more than three tricks:

DUMMY: ◆ A K Q 3 2

DECLARER: ◆ 6 5 4

You plan to play the Ace, King and Queen and hope that the opponents' cards will divide 3-2 and your remaining two cards will be winners. Even if the suit breaks 4-1, you can lead the suit again, giving a trick to the opponents, and establishing your remaining card as a winner. But suppose you have this situation:

DUMMY: ♥ A K J 3 2

DECLARER: ♥ 6 5 4

Should you play the Ace and the King, trying to develop the suit through length, or should you take the finesse? In this chapter we'll see how the popular maxim **eight ever, nine never** helps you decide what to do in such situations.

Eight Ever

Look at this combination of cards:

DUMMY: ◆ A 6 5 3

DECLARER: ◆ K J 4 2

Suppose you want to take all four tricks in this suit. How do you go about it? You are missing the Queen and there are two possible ways to avoid losing a trick to it. First, you can take a trick with the Ace and a trick with the King, hoping that one of the opponents started with a doubleton Queen and will have to play it. Now you can take a trick with the Jack, and since the opponents' cards have broken 3-2, your remaining small card is also a winner.

The alternative is to take a trick with the Ace and then lead a small card toward your hand, intending to finesse the Jack if East plays a small card. You have to hope that East started with the Queen. If the finesse works and West plays a small card, the suit will have broken 3-2 and you can play the King to take care of East's Queen. The remaining small card also will be a winner.

Which is the better choice? The first part of the maxim offers you some useful advice: **eight ever**. With eight cards in the combined hands, missing the Queen, it is usually best to take the finesse. "Ever" is a bit extreme, because there may be extenuating circumstances when the whole hand is taken into consideration, but it provides a guideline when you have nothing better to go on.

Here is a similar situation:

DUMMY: ♥ K 5

DECLARER: ♥ A J 8 7 6 4

To try and take the maximum number of tricks in this suit, start by playing dummy's King (high card from the short side) and leading dummy's Five toward your hand. If East plays small cards both times, finesse the Jack because you have eight cards in the combined hands. You are hoping that the complete distribution resembles this layout:

♥ K 5

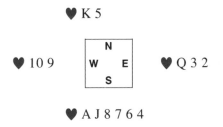

♥ 10 9   ♥ Q 3 2

♥ A J 8 7 6 4

You would be unlucky if the cards were actually distributed as shown on the next page, because, had you played the King, followed by the Ace, avoiding the finesse, you would have taken all six tricks in Hearts. By trying the finesse, you can take only five tricks. The reason the maxim is sound is not that it works all the time, but that it wins more often than it loses.

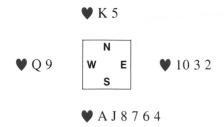

However, one of the advantages of taking the finesse is that it will save you a trick if the suit breaks unfavorably:

If you don't take the finesse in this situation, you will lose two tricks in the suit.

Here's an example in a complete hand:

Contract: Six No Trump

West leads ♥10

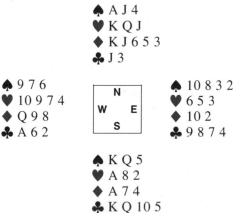

You need to take twelve tricks. You start with three Spade winners, three Heart winners and two Diamond winners. You can promote three Club winners by driving out the opponents' Ace, but you will still need one extra trick from the Diamond suit. Should you plan to play the Ace and the King, hoping that the Queen will be singleton or doubleton?

You have eight Diamonds in the combined hands. Eight ever tells you that your best chance is to take the Diamond finesse. This advice succeeds with the above hand and in addition to driving out the opponents' Ace of Clubs, gives you enough winners to make your slam contract.

More About Eight Ever

Some of the principles we have seen in earlier chapters are combined with the concept of eight ever. For example, look at this combination:

DUMMY: ♣ A K J 3

DECLARER: ♣ 7 6 4 2

With eight cards, you plan to take the finesse by leading toward dummy's Jack. However, if you have sufficient entries, you can afford to play dummy's Ace or King first. This strategy protects you against losses if the opponents' cards are distributed in the following fashion:

♣ A K J 3

```
         N
♣ 10 9 8 5   W   E   ♣ Q
         S
```

♣ 7 6 4 2

If you take the Ace and East plays a small card rather than the Queen, come back to your hand in another suit and take the finesse.

In this situation, you must be more careful:

DUMMY: ♦ A K J 10 6 4

DECLARER: ♦ 7 3

With eight cards, you are planning to take the finesse. It may seem a good idea to play the Ace or the King first in case East has a singleton Queen. But what if this is the complete layout?

♦ A K J 10 6 4

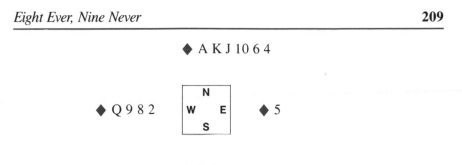

♦ Q 9 8 2   ♦ 5

♦ 7 3

If you play one of dummy's high cards first, you can no longer play the suit without losing a trick. Contrast this result with that of taking a finesse right away. When it works, you can come back to your hand and repeat the finesse. You end up taking all the tricks in the suit. Since it is more likely that East has the singleton Nine, Eight, Five or Two than specifically the singleton Queen, you should not play a high card first unless you do not have sufficient entries to take two finesses.

Here is a situation in which you can preserve an entry by leading a high card:

DUMMY: ♠ A K J 5

DECLARER: ♠ 10 9 6 3

If you are in your hand and have no more entries, you should lead the Ten (or the Nine) from your hand rather than a small card. This will help if the complete distribution of the suit is as follows:

♠ A K J 5

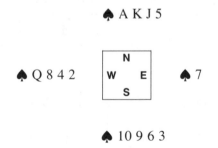

♠ Q 8 4 2   ♠ 7

♠ 10 9 6 3

You can afford to lead the Ten, since if West covers with the Queen, you have the Ace, King, Jack and Nine to take all of the tricks. If West plays a small card, play a small card from dummy. When the Ten wins the trick, you are still in your hand and can repeat the finesse. If you started by playing a small card to dummy's Jack, the finesse would work, but you would be in the wrong hand to repeat it.

Here is an example from a complete hand:

Contract: Three No Trump

West leads ♠K

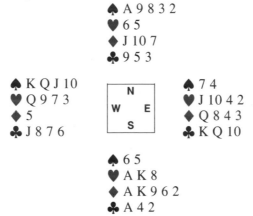

```
                        ♠ A 9 8 3 2
                        ♥ 6 5
                        ♦ J 10 7
                        ♣ 9 5 3
   ♠ K Q J 10                              ♠ 7 4
   ♥ Q 9 7 3          N                    ♥ J 10 4 2
   ♦ 5            W         E              ♦ Q 8 4 3
   ♣ J 8 7 6              S                ♣ K Q 10
                        ♠ 6 5
                        ♥ A K 8
                        ♦ A K 9 6 2
                        ♣ A 4 2
```

You need nine winners and start with six: one Spade, two Hearts, two Diamonds and one Club. The extra tricks can come from the Diamond suit, but you are missing the Queen. With eight cards, you plan to take a finesse.

West's lead will drive out dummy's only entry, so be careful to lead the Jack (or the Ten) of Diamonds from dummy. If East plays a small card, you will still be in dummy when the finesse works and can repeat it by leading the Ten. If East covers the Jack with the Queen, win the Ace and play a small Diamond to dummy's Ten (high card from the short side). Next, play dummy's remaining Diamond to the winners in your hand and you will have taken nine tricks.

When you have eight cards and are missing the Queen, you can only apply **eight ever** if there is an opportunity to finesse. Look at this combination of cards:

DUMMY: ♥ J 6 5 3

DECLARER: ♥ A K 4 2

You have eight cards in the combined hands, but as you saw in the previous chapter, you cannot afford to lead dummy's Jack to take a finesse. Even if East has the Queen, it will do no good, because East will cover the Jack with the Queen, forcing you to play the Ace or the King to take the trick. Since your side does not have the Ten, the opponents will take a trick even if the suit breaks 3-2. Instead, you must play the Ace and the King and hope that one of the opponents has to play the Queen. Here is a similar situation:

DUMMY: ♣ A K 7 4 2

DECLARER: ♣ J 6 3

Without the Ten, you cannot take a finesse. If you need all the tricks, you will have to play the Ace and the King and hope that one of the opponents started with a doubleton Queen.

Sometimes, you have a choice of which opponent to play for the Queen, a two-way finesse:

DUMMY: ♠ K 10 7 3

DECLARER: ♠ A J 5 4

You have eight cards and are just missing the Queen, so **eight ever** applies. But you can decide whether to play East or West for the Queen. If you think East has the Queen, play a small card to dummy's King and lead a small card toward your hand, intending to finesse the Jack if East plays a small card. If you think West has the Queen, play the Ace first and lead a small card toward dummy, intending to finesse the Ten if West plays a small card. As was pointed out in the previous chapter, you often have to guess, but sometimes there is a clue from the bidding or the play.

Here is an example in which it is safer to finesse in one direction than the other:

Contract: Three No Trump

West leads ♠4

```
                    ♠ 10 7 6
                    ♥ K Q 3
                    ♦ A 10 6 4
                    ♣ K 8 5

    ♠ K J 9 4 2       ┌───────┐      ♠ Q 8
    ♥ 9 4 2           │   N   │      ♥ J 8 7 6
    ♦ Q 7 2        W  │       │  E   ♦ 9 8
    ♣ 10 2            │   S   │      ♣ Q J 7 6 4
                      └───────┘
                    ♠ A 5 3
                    ♥ A 10 5
                    ♦ K J 5 3
                    ♣ A 9 3
```

You need nine winners and start with eight: one Spade, three Hearts, two Diamonds and two Clubs. Your ninth winner can come from the Diamond suit through a successful finesse against the Queen. Your Diamond holding is such that you have a choice as to which opponent to play for the Queen.

West has led a Spade, putting the contract in some danger. Once your Ace has been played, if you let the opponents in with the Queen of Diamonds, they may be able to take enough tricks to defeat the contract. To protect yourself as much as possible, you make use of the hold-up play. Let East win the first trick with the Queen of Spades and play a small card again when the suit is led. When West leads the suit for a third time, you must use the Ace, but now you can see that East has no Spades left. You have successfully removed all of East's link cards.

This helps you decide which way to take the finesse. Since West is the dangerous opponent, you plan to take the finesse to avoid giving West an opportunity to win the trick. After winning with the Ace of Spades, play the King of Diamonds and a small Diamond toward dummy. When West plays a small card, you finesse dummy's Ten.

This plan succeeds on the actual hand and you make an overtrick. However, your contract would still be safe if East had won the trick. East is not the dangerous opponent and now your Jack has been promoted into the extra winner you need. Contrast this result with that of taking the finesse in the other direction. When it loses to West's Queen, West takes the rest of the Spade tricks and your contract is defeated.

Nine Never

Let's take a look at this combination of cards:

DUMMY: ♥ A 6 5 3

DECLARER: ♥ K J 7 4 2

Once again, the Queen is missing, but this time, there are nine cards in the combined hands. If you play a small card to dummy's Ace and lead a small card back to your hand, what should you do when East plays a small card? Now the second part of the maxim, **nine never**, provides some advice. When you start with nine cards and there is nothing better to guide you, play the King and do not take the finesse.

This may seem a bit strange since when the opponents have four cards, they are more likely to break 3-1 than 2-2. However, when you play the Ace and a small card toward your King and East plays a small card, you have already eliminated the possibility that the suit broke 4-0 or 3-1 with

West having the three cards. This tips the scale slightly in favor of playing the King and hoping the suit breaks 2-2. Hence the maxim **nine never**. Again, "never" is a bit strong, as we shall see in the next chapter, but the idea is sound.

Here is a similar situation:

DUMMY: ♣ A K J 8 7

DECLARER: ♣ 9 6 4 2

Rather than taking a finesse, you should play the Ace and the King, hoping that the suit is divided in the following fashion:

♣ A K J 8 7

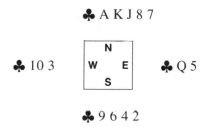

♣ 10 3   ♣ Q 5

♣ 9 6 4 2

This would also work if it turned out that the suit was originally distributed like this, since it wouldn't matter whether you tried the finesse or played the Ace followed by the King:

♣ A K J 8 7

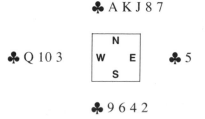

♣ Q 5   ♣ 10 3

♣ 9 6 4 2

You would be unlucky if it turned out that the suit was originally distributed like this:

♣ A K J 8 7

♣ Q 10 3   ♣ 5

♣ 9 6 4 2

Let's take a look at this concept in a complete hand:

Contract: Two Spades

West leads ◆Q

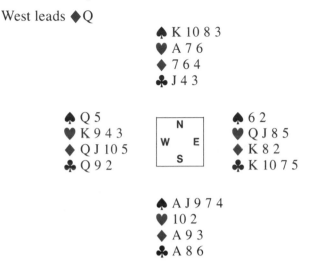

                    ♠ K 10 8 3
                    ♥ A 7 6
                    ◆ 7 6 4
                    ♣ J 4 3

♠ Q 5   ♠ 6 2
♥ K 9 4 3   N   ♥ Q J 8 5
◆ Q J 10 5   W   E   ◆ K 8 2
♣ Q 9 2   S   ♣ K 10 7 5

                    ♠ A J 9 7 4
                    ♥ 10 2
                    ◆ A 9 3
                    ♣ A 8 6

You can afford five losers. You are missing the Queen of Spades and have a Heart loser, two Diamond losers and two Club losers. There's not much to be done about the losers in Hearts, Diamonds and Clubs, so you must concentrate on avoiding the Spade loser.

You could take a finesse, and with the Ten in dummy and the Jack in your hand, you could finesse either opponent for the Queen. However, with nine cards in the combined hands, you can make use of nine never and just play the Ace and the King, hoping that the suit breaks 2-2 or that one opponent started with a singleton Queen. In the above hand, this plan will work and you will make your contract.

Here is a more dramatic example. We'll keep the East and West hands hidden for a moment to give you the feeling that you would have as declarer.

Contract: Seven No Trump

♠ A Q J
♥ A Q 5
◆ K J 9
♣ K J 10 8

```
        N
West leads ♥J   W    E
        S
```

♠ K 9 8
♥ K 9
◆ A Q 6
♣ A 9 6 4 3

You need all thirteen tricks and you start with eleven: three Spades, three Hearts, three Diamonds and two Clubs. You have no choice but to try and get the extra tricks from the Club suit. Eventually, you play the Ace, on which West plays the Two and East plays the Five. You lead a small card and West produces the Seven. Now what?

The maxim in this chapter—eight ever, nine never—will take a lot of the pressure off. With nine cards in the combined hands, this advice warns you not to finesse—so play dummy's King and hold your breath! On this hand, you are amply rewarded when the full layout turns out to be as follows:

♠ A Q J
♥ A Q 5
◆ K J 9
♣ K J 10 8

♠ 7 5 3 2   ♠ 10 6 4
♥ J 10 8 4   ♥ 7 6 3 2
◆ 10 8 4   ◆ 7 5 3 2
♣ 7 2   ♣ Q 5

```
        N
    W       E
        S
```

♠ K 9 8
♥ K 9
◆ A Q 6
♣ A 9 6 4 3

Summary

When missing the Queen in a long suit, you often have a choice between playing the Ace and the King (hoping one of the opponents will have to play the Queen) or taking a finesse when you have the Jack. The following maxim provides a useful guideline:

KEY MAXIM

Eight Ever, Nine Never

This advice reminds you that, without any other information to guide you, you should finesse if you have eight cards or less, but play the Ace and the King if you have nine or more.

Exercises

1) You are in a contract of Three No Trump. How do you plan to play it?

♠ 10 6 3
♥ K 9 5
♦ A 7 4
♣ K 7 4 3

West leads ♦Q

```
      N
  W       E
      S
```

♠ A 8 7
♥ A 6 3
♦ K 5 2
♣ A J 8 5

Solution

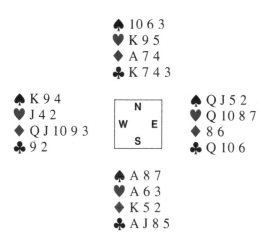

♠ 10 6 3
♥ K 9 5
♦ A 7 4
♣ K 7 4 3

♠ K 9 4
♥ J 4 2
♦ Q J 10 9 3
♣ 9 2

♠ Q J 5 2
♥ Q 10 8 7
♦ 8 6
♣ Q 10 6

♠ A 8 7
♥ A 6 3
♦ K 5 2
♣ A J 8 5

You need nine winners. You have one sure Spade trick, two Heart tricks, two Diamond Tricks and two Club tricks. You need to find two more tricks. The only hope appears to be in the Club suit. You will need to take all four tricks.

Eight ever, nine never tells you to try the finesse rather than playing the Ace and the King. Take a trick with dummy's King of Clubs first, in case West started with a singleton Queen, but then lead a small Club toward your hand and when East follows with a small card, finesse the Jack.

In the actual hand, the finesse works and the Club suit divides 3-2, so you finish with nine tricks.

2) You are in a contract of Four Hearts. How will the maxim eight ever, nine never help you make the contract?

♠ A 7 3
♥ K 9 2
♦ A 10 6 4
♣ K Q 5

West leads ♠5

```
      N
  W       E
      S
```

♠ 8 4 2
♥ A J 8 7 5 3
♦ K 3
♣ 7 2

Solution

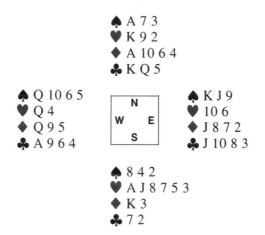

♠ A 7 3
♥ K 9 2
♦ A 10 6 4
♣ K Q 5

♠ Q 10 6 5
♥ Q 4
♦ Q 9 5
♣ A 9 6 4

♠ K J 9
♥ 10 6
♦ J 8 7 2
♣ J 10 8 3

♠ 8 4 2
♥ A J 8 7 5 3
♦ K 3
♣ 7 2

You can afford three losers. You have two Spade losers, a potential Heart loser and a Club loser. You might consider leading twice toward dummy's King and Queen of Clubs. If West has the Ace, you can establish an extra winner in dummy on which to discard a loser. However, that plan won't work because the opponents have already led a Spade. Once you take your Ace, the opponents will be able to take two Spade tricks when they get in with the Ace of Clubs before you have an opportunity to discard one.

Instead, you must plan to avoid losing a Heart trick. With nine cards in the combined hands, the maxim indicates that you should not take the finesse. After winning the Ace of Spades, play the Ace and the King of Hearts and hope that the Queen is singleton or doubleton.

3) You reach a contract of Two Spades. West leads the Jack of Hearts and the opponents immediately take the first three Heart tricks. They now lead a Diamond. Are you still going to make your contract?

♠ A 6 3
♥ Q 8 3
♦ K 9 6
♣ 8 7 5 2

West leads ♥J

	N	
W		E
	S	

♠ K J 7 5 2
♥ 7 6 5
♦ A 8 3
♣ A 10

Solution

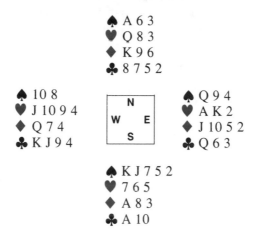

```
              ♠ A 6 3
              ♥ Q 8 3
              ♦ K 9 6
              ♣ 8 7 5 2
♠ 10 8                         ♠ Q 9 4
♥ J 10 9 4                     ♥ A K 2
♦ Q 7 4                        ♦ J 10 5 2
♣ K J 9 4                      ♣ Q 6 3
              ♠ K J 7 5 2
              ♥ 7 6 5
              ♦ A 8 3
              ♣ A 10
```

You can afford five losers. You have three Heart losers, a Diamond loser and a Club loser. In addition, you are missing the Queen of the trump suit. There are no obvious ways to eliminate your losers, so you are going to have to take all the Spade tricks.

With eight cards, the maxim advises you to take the finesse. As soon as you win a trick, play a Spade to dummy's Ace and a small Spade back toward your hand. If East produces the Queen, all is well. If East plays a small card, play the Jack from your hand and keep your fingers crossed.

12

Eight Ever, Nine Never . . . The Other Side of the Coin

Eight ever, nine never tells you the best way to handle an eight- or nine-card suit missing the Queen, all else being equal. With eight cards you should finesse for the Queen, if possible; with nine cards you should not take the finesse.

However, as with all the bridge maxims, there are exceptions to the rule. You must look at the overall plan for making the contract before you can decide on the best way to play a particular suit. Sometimes taking a finesse with eight cards will jeopardize the contract. Sometimes not taking the finesse with nine cards will also court disaster. In this chapter, we'll look at some of the danger signals that help you decide when to apply and when to set aside this maxim.

Avoiding the Dangerous Opponent

Making the contract has a higher priority than playing an individual suit for the maximum number of tricks—this is especially true when you are trying to avoid a dangerous opponent. There are many hands in which you can afford to lose a trick in a suit, but you want to lose it to the safe opponent, not to the dangerous one.

Here is an example:

Contract: Three No Trump

West leads ◆K

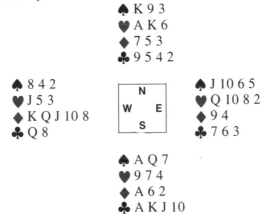

```
                      ♠ K 9 3
                      ♥ A K 6
                      ◆ 7 5 3
                      ♣ 9 5 4 2

  ♠ 8 4 2                        ♠ J 10 6 5
  ♥ J 5 3          N             ♥ Q 10 8 2
  ◆ K Q J 10 8   W   E           ◆ 9 4
  ♣ Q 8            S             ♣ 7 6 3

                      ♠ A Q 7
                      ♥ 9 7 4
                      ◆ A 6 2
                      ♣ A K J 10
```

You need nine winners. You have three Spade tricks, two Heart tricks, one Diamond trick and two Club tricks. One more trick must be developed. The only suit that provides this opportunity is Clubs. You have eight of them, missing the Queen, and would normally plan to take a finesse.

However, in putting it all together, you discover a problem. West has led a Diamond and, once the Ace is gone, if the opponents win a trick, they may be in a position to take enough tricks to defeat the contract.

You can prevent that outcome by employing the hold-up play. You don't plan to win the first or even the second Diamond trick, but wait until the third round of the suit. That delay should be more than sufficient to remove East's link cards in the suit. Now East will be a safe opponent and West will be the dangerous opponent.

The problem with taking the Club finesse is that, if it doesn't work, it will be West who wins the trick, a situation that you want to prevent. You don't mind losing a Club trick to East because you only need one more trick to make the contract, not two. How can you best guard against West winning a trick?

The answer is to play the Ace and the King of Clubs first and then play the Jack (or the Ten) to drive out the Queen. This strategy will stop West from winning a Club trick unless West has three or more Clubs, including the Queen. Look at the effect in the actual hand. If it turns out that East had three or more Clubs, including the Queen, you will lose an overtrick but still make the contract.

Here is a more difficult example involving the same concept:

Contract: Four Hearts

West leads ♦J

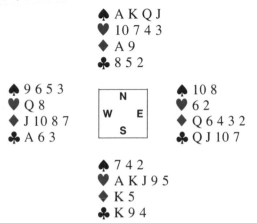

```
                    ♠ A K Q J
                    ♥ 10 7 4 3
                    ♦ A 9
                    ♣ 8 5 2

  ♠ 9 6 5 3           N           ♠ 10 8
  ♥ Q 8                           ♥ 6 2
  ♦ J 10 8 7     W       E        ♦ Q 6 4 3 2
  ♣ A 6 3             S           ♣ Q J 10 7

                    ♠ 7 4 2
                    ♥ A K J 9 5
                    ♦ K 5
                    ♣ K 9 4
```

You can afford three losers. You have no losers in Spades or Diamonds, but the Queen of Hearts is missing and there are three possible Club losers. With nine cards in Hearts, normal play is to take the Ace and the King, hoping that one of the opponents must play the Queen. As you can see from looking at the actual hand, in this instance the normal play is effective, and you have no problem making the contract. However, there is more to this hand, and unlikely as it may seem, the correct play is to take a Heart finesse even though it loses to West's Queen!

To understand why, you must take a closer look at the entire hand, and especially at the possibilities for eliminating the Club losers. There are two ways to avoid losing all three Club tricks. You can lead a Club from dummy toward the King and hope that East has the Ace or you can discard one of your Club losers on dummy's extra Spade winner. The first method requires that a specific card, the Ace, be favorably located. The second is a sure thing, provided that all the opponents' trump is drawn first.

Since discarding the Club loser is a sure way to make the contract, it would seem that you should just plan to draw trump and then discard your loser. But there is a danger. If East started with three Hearts, including the Queen, and has an opportunity to lead while you are drawing trump, East is a dangerous opponent. East can lead a Club and if West has the Ace, your King will be trapped. You will lose three Club tricks in addition to the trump trick. On the other hand, if you lose a trump trick to West, there is no such danger. West can take the Ace of Clubs, but your King will be able to win the next trick. After drawing any remaining trump, you can safely discard your other Club loser on the extra Spade winner.

The safest plan is to win the first trick with the King of Diamonds and take the Ace (or the King) of Hearts in case one of the opponents has a singleton Queen. If the Queen does not appear, use one of your entries to dummy to lead a Heart toward your hand, and plan to play the Jack if East plays a small card. On the actual hand, you will lose to West's Queen, but now all the trump will be drawn and West can do you no damage. You will be able to discard your Club loser and make the contract.

By taking a finesse even though you have nine cards in the suit, you protect the contract in case the actual layout resembles the following:

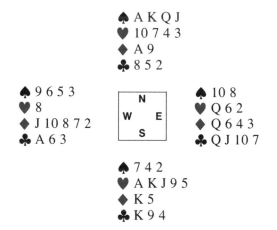

If you win the Diamond and play the Ace and the King of Hearts, East still has the Queen left. Even if you leave East with the Queen while you try to discard your Club loser, it won't work. East will trump the third Spade trick with the Queen of Hearts and lead the Queen of Clubs, trapping the King. Down you go!

Preventing Disaster

One of the dangers in a suit contract is that the opponents might use their trump to trump your winners. This is why you usually get the kiddies off the street as soon as possible. Therefore, you must think twice before playing eight ever in a trump contract.

Look at this example:

Contract: Four Spades

West leads ♣4

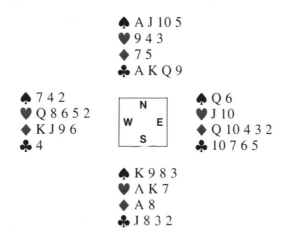

```
                      ♠ A J 10 5
                      ♥ 9 4 3
                      ♦ 7 5
                      ♣ A K Q 9

  ♠ 7 4 2                              ♠ Q 6
  ♥ Q 8 6 5 2          N              ♥ J 10
  ♦ K J 9 6        W       E          ♦ Q 10 4 3 2
  ♣ 4                  S              ♣ 10 7 6 5

                      ♠ K 9 8 3
                      ♥ A K 7
                      ♦ A 8
                      ♣ J 8 3 2
```

You can afford three losers. You are missing the Queen of Spades and you have a Heart loser and a Diamond loser. It looks as though you will make your contract even if you lose a trick to the Queen of Spades.

The danger here is that you can afford one loser in the trump suit, but you cannot afford two losers. If you try to take a finesse and it happens to lose to the Queen, the opponents still have a trump left. They may be able to use it to trump one of your winners, producing an unexpected loser.

In the actual hand, if you win the first Club trick and play a Spade to the King, followed by a small Spade to dummy's Jack (taking a finesse because you have eight cards in the combined hands) the contract suddenly strikes a reef! East leads another Club and West trumps with the remaining small Spade. You still have to lose the Heart and Diamond tricks.

The safe play is to use the Ace and the King of Spades first. If the Queen doesn't appear, you can afford to lose a trick to it. That will be the only Spade loser. On the actual hand, the Queen will appear and you will make an overtrick . . . your just reward for taking the time to plan out the play of the entire hand rather than concentrating on the Spade suit alone.

Here is an example in which blind adherence to eight ever, nine never could lead to disaster in a No Trump contract:

Contract: One No Trump

West leads ♥Q

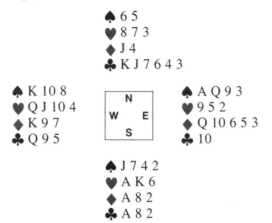

```
                   ♠ 6 5
                   ♥ 8 7 3
                   ♦ J 4
                   ♣ K J 7 6 4 3
♠ K 10 8                            ♠ A Q 9 3
♥ Q J 10 4        N                ♥ 9 5 2
♦ K 9 7       W       E            ♦ Q 10 6 5 3
♣ Q 9 5           S                ♣ 10
                   ♠ J 7 4 2
                   ♥ A K 6
                   ♦ A 8 2
                   ♣ A 8 2
```

You need seven winners. There are two sure tricks in Hearts, one in Diamonds and two in Clubs. The two extra tricks will have to come from the Club suit. Normally, with a nine-card suit that is missing the Queen, you would remember nine never, and plan to play the Ace and the King.

There are two conflicting ideas in this hand. The maxim, eight ever, nine never, suggests that the best way to play the Club suit is to play the Ace and the King, and hope that the Queen falls. However, there is another consideration to be seen when you look at the whole hand. You must watch your entries. As you have seen in previous examples, a long suit is of no value if it is stranded. The only entry you have in dummy is in the Club suit. You need to save a link card to get over to the Club winners. You might think of trying the finesse as a ducking play. You don't care if the finesse loses; your aim is to take your losses early so that, when your Clubs are set up, you are in dummy.

To guard against this disaster, after winning the first Heart trick and playing the Ace of Clubs, play a small Club and finesse dummy's Jack. If it loses to East's Queen, you still have enough winners to make the contract with an overtrick. If the finesse wins, you end up with two overtricks. Either way, "nine ever" turns out to be the correct play for this hand.

Entry Problems

The previous hand stressed the importance of watching your entries when planning the play. Here is another example:

Contract: One No Trump

West leads ♥K

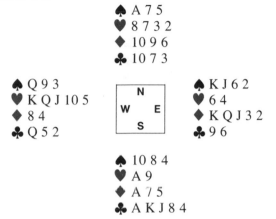

```
              ♠ A 7 5
              ♥ 8 7 3 2
              ♦ 10 9 6
              ♣ 10 7 3
♠ Q 9 3                        ♠ K J 6 2
♥ K Q J 10 5     N             ♥ 6 4
♦ 8 4        W       E         ♦ K Q J 3 2
♣ Q 5 2          S             ♣ 9 6
              ♠ 10 8 4
              ♥ A 9
              ♦ A 7 5
              ♣ A K J 8 4
```

You start with five of the seven winners you need: one Spade, one Diamond, one Heart and two Clubs. The extra tricks can be developed in the Club suit. It would be nice to take a finesse, hoping East has the Queen, because you have eight Clubs.

However, the only entry to dummy is the Ace of Spades. It would be dangerous to play a small Spade to dummy's Ace if it is not necessary. West has led Hearts, and even if you hold up, the opponents will be ready to take some Heart tricks, should they get the opportunity. If you play your only winner in the Spade suit, the opponents will also be able to take some Spade tricks if the Club finesse loses. The combined Heart and Spade tricks, in addition to the Queen of Clubs, may be enough for the opponents to defeat your contract.

You do not need all five tricks in the Club suit; it will be enough if you can take four tricks. Since you can afford to lose a trick to the opponents' Queen, play the Ace and the King and if necessary, drive out the Queen. The opponents can take some Heart tricks when they win the Queen of Clubs, but not enough to defeat the contract. You will be able to take seven tricks.

One last example:

Contract: Three No Trump

West leads ♠Q

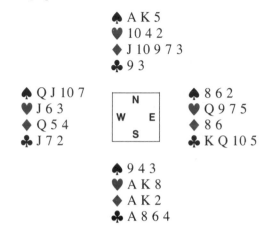

♠ A K 5
♥ 10 4 2
♦ J 10 9 7 3
♣ 9 3

♠ Q J 10 7
♥ J 6 3
♦ Q 5 4
♣ J 7 2

♠ 8 6 2
♥ Q 9 7 5
♦ 8 6
♣ K Q 10 5

♠ 9 4 3
♥ A K 8
♦ A K 2
♣ A 8 6 4

You need nine tricks. There are two sure tricks in Spades, two in Hearts, two in Diamonds and one in Clubs, for a total of seven. You need to develop two extra tricks and it should be possible to establish these in the Diamond suit.

If you try the Diamond finesse and it loses, West will no doubt lead another Spade, removing dummy's last entry before you are ready. You can play the Ace and the King of Diamonds, but now you are in your hand and dummy's two Diamond winners are stranded.

Play the Ace and the King of Diamonds. Then lead the Two of Diamonds to dummy's Jack (or Ten or Nine) to drive out the Queen. Now you have developed two extra tricks in Diamonds and you still have a Spade winner left as an entry.

Summary

The maxim eight ever, nine never is useful when deciding on the best play in an individual suit. However, you may have to ignore this advice on a particular hand when it would endanger the contract.

You must always develop your plan for the entire hand before you start. Keep your objective in mind, determine how far you are from it and what you need to do to reach it. In putting it all together, you may find that a particular maxim is useful or, alternatively, that it doesn't apply in your present situation.

Exercises

1) You are in a contract of Three No Trump. You will need an extra trick from the Club suit. Is this a case of eight ever?

♠ K 10 5
♥ 5 4 2
♦ A 8 3
♣ A 7 5 2

West leads ♥7

```
      N
  W       E
      S
```

♠ A 8 2
♥ A 10 9
♦ K Q 4
♣ K J 6 3

Solution

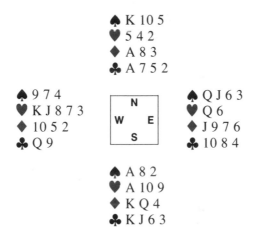

♠ K 10 5
♥ 5 4 2
♦ A 8 3
♣ A 7 5 2

♠ 9 7 4
♥ K J 8 7 3
♦ 10 5 2
♣ Q 9

♠ Q J 6 3
♥ Q 6
♦ J 9 7 6
♣ 10 8 4

♠ A 8 2
♥ A 10 9
♦ K Q 4
♣ K J 6 3

You need nine winners. You have two Spade tricks, one Heart trick, three Diamond tricks and two Club tricks. One more trick will see you safely home. The Club suit has the potential to produce extra tricks, and with eight cards in the combined hands, you would normally plan to take a finesse.

However, West has led Hearts. Therefore, once you have won the Ace, the opponents will be able to take their Heart winners if the finesse loses and they take the lead. You can improve your chances by holding up the Heart Ace until the third round. Hopefully that play will remove any link cards in Hearts from East's hand to make East a safe opponent.

You only need one extra trick in the Club suit. West is the dangerous opponent, so you want to avoid losing a trick to West if possible. Play the King and the Ace of Clubs. If the Queen has not appeared, lead another Club and hope that East wins it. Only if West has three or more Clubs, including the Queen, will the contract be in danger.

2) Again you are in Three No Trump. West has led your weakest suit, so you plan to hold up twice before taking your Ace to try eliminating East's link cards. But then it will be time to tackle the Diamond suit. Is this the time for nine never or are there other factors involved?

♠ 8 7
♥ 9 6
♦ A J 10 7 5 3
♣ A 7 6

West leads ♠ K

	N	
W		E
	S	

♠ A 6 2
♥ A K 5 3
♦ K 9 2
♣ K 5 2

Solution

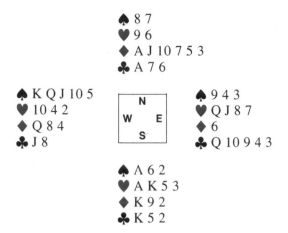

You need nine tricks. You have one Spade trick, two Heart tricks, two Diamond tricks and two Club tricks. The extra tricks will have to come from the Diamond suit. With nine cards, missing the Queen, you would normally play the Ace and the King first.

However, West has led Spades and will drive out your Ace. You can hold up the first two tricks, but you must win the third. West is likely to have the long Spades and is, therefore, a dangerous opponent. East is not dangerous. If East has a Spade left, the suit will have originally been divided 4-4 and the opponents cannot take more than three tricks in Spades. So it is safe to lose a Diamond trick to East, but not to West.

After winning the Ace of Spades, play the King of Diamonds, followed by a small Diamond toward dummy. If West plays a small card, finesse the Jack (or the Ten). If it loses to East's Queen, your contract is safe. If the finesse works, as it does in the actual hand, you have all the Diamond tricks and have made two overtricks.

3) You reach a contract of Four Hearts. You are going to start by drawing trump, but can you afford to take the Heart finesse?

♠ A J 7
♥ K 6 3
♦ A 9 7 6 2
♣ 8 5

West leads ♦ J

```
    N
W       E
    S
```

♠ 9 3
♥ A J 10 9 8
♦ K Q 8 4 3
♣ J

Solution

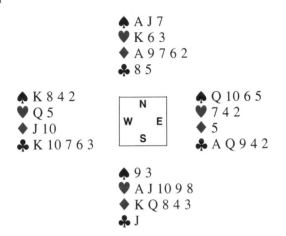

♠ A J 7
♥ K 6 3
♦ A 9 7 6 2
♣ 8 5

♠ K 8 4 2
♥ Q 5
♦ J 10
♣ K 10 7 6 3

♠ Q 10 6 5
♥ 7 4 2
♦ 5
♣ A Q 9 4 2

♠ 9 3
♥ A J 10 9 8
♦ K Q 8 4 3
♣ J

You can afford three losers. You have a Spade loser, a potential Heart loser and a Club loser. The contract looks safe enough, so you should start by drawing trump.

With eight Hearts, not including the Queen, you could take a finesse—but that would put the contract in danger. You can afford one loser in the trump suit, but not two. Play the Ace and the King of Hearts. Even if the Queen does not appear, that is the only Heart trick you will lose.

On the actual hand, if you take a Heart finesse that loses to West's Queen, West can lead another Diamond, which East will trump to defeat the contract.

Glossary

AGAINST You finesse against a card by trying to trap it with a finesse.

BREAK The division of a suit between the opponents' hands. (See also: **split.**)

BUILD Set up sure tricks by driving out winning cards in the opponents' hands. (See also: **establish, develop.**)

COMBINED Including the declarer and the dummy.

CONTROL Deciding when to let the opponents take the lead.

DANGEROUS OPPONENT A defender is dangerous if he can, or might, be able to lead a card that will set your contract.

DECLARER The person playing the contract, in this book South is always assumed to be declarer and is often referred to as "you" (the reader).

DISCARD The play to a trick of a card of a different suit, not trump, than the suit led.

DISTRIBUTION The number of cards held in each suit by a particular player; the number of cards held in a particular suit by a partnership; the way in which the cards of a particular suit are divided among the four players.

DOUBLETON A holding of two cards in a suit.

DRAWING TRUMP Playing the trump suit until the opponents have none left.

DRIVE OUT The defenders' winner in a suit is driven out if you keep leading the suit until they have to play their winner.

ENTRY A card that provides a means of winning a trick in a particular hand.

ESTABLISH Set up sure tricks by driving out winning cards in the opponents' hands. (See also: **build, develop.**)

EVENLY Refers to the distribution of a suit among two hands of a partnership where both players have the same number of cards in the suit. For example, if declarer and dummy both have four Diamonds, Diamonds are divided evenly.

FAVORABLE DISTRIBUTION A distribution of the opponents' cards in a suit that gives the declarer the best chance to make the contract.

FAVORABLE POSITION The critical card(s) are held by the desired opponent, allowing the declarer to take a successful finesse.

FINESSE A method of building extra tricks by trapping an opponent's high high card(s).

GIVE UP THE LEAD Allowing the opponents to win a trick.

HAND Generally the cards held by one of the players; often the cards held by the declarer as opposed to the dummy.

HIGH CARD One of the top five cards in a suit: Ace, King, Queen, Jack, Ten. In the bidding only the top four cards are given points.

HOLD-UP (PLAY) Refusing to take a winner at your first opportunity, the idea being to remove one opponent's link cards in that suit.

HONOR (CARD) An Ace, King, Queen, Jack or Ten.

LAYOUT The way the unseen cards held by the opponents were dealt.

LINK CARD A card which can be led to a winner (entry) in the opposite hand.

LOSER A trick which the declarer could lose: a quick loser is one that the declarer will lose as soon as he gives up the lead; a slow loser is one that declarer may eventually lose.

OPENING LEAD The first card played. The opening lead is made by the defender on the declarer's left.

ORDER Signifying the cards played and the order they are played in. For example with ♦ K 2, it may be better to play the King, then the Two, instead of the Two before the King.

OUTSTANDING The cards in a suit that have not yet been played.

OVERTAKE Playing a bigger card on partner's winning card. A rare play used when you have extra high cards, but not enough entries.

OVERTRICK An extra trick beyond what declarer needs to achieve his objective (make his contract.)

PROMOTE The increase in the trick-taking potential of a card in a suit as the higher-ranking cards are played.

REPEATED FINESSE A finesse that you need to take two (or more) times to complete successfully.

RUFF Playing trump on a trick when you are void in the suit led. (See also: **trump**).

RUN Taking the rest of the tricks in a suit (by one team, declarer or the defenders.)

SAFE OPPONENT A safe defender cannot set your contract if he gains the lead.

SET THE CONTRACT The defenders set the contract when they take enough tricks to prevent declarer from reaching his objective.

SEQUENCE   Three or more cards of the same suit in consecutive order of rank. Examples: King-Queen-Jack; Queen-Jack-Ten-Nine.

SHOW OUT   The failure of a defender to follow to a suit led by declarer or dummy.

SINGLETON   A holding of one card in a suit.

SMALL CARD   A low card in a suit, which is unlikely to have any trick-taking potential.

SPLIT   The division of a suit between the opponents' hands. (See also: **break**.)

STRANDED   Winners in a suit are stranded when they cannot be taken because there are no entries to them.

SURE TRICK   A trick which can be taken without giving up the lead to the opponents.

TAKE THE LEAD   A player who wins a trick led by a different player is said to take the lead for the next trick.

THROW AWAY   See **discard**.

TIMING   The art of playing the right cards at the right time.

TOWARD   A play from the opposite hand to that which holds the high card(s).

TWO-WAY FINESSE   A situation in which you could play either defender for the missing high card. Almost always arises when the missing card is the Queen and you have the Ace, King, Jack and Ten, with the Ace (or King) in dummy and the King (or Ace) in your hand.

UNEVENLY   Refers to the distribution of a suit among the two hands of a partnership, where the players have unequal length in the suit.

UNFAVORABLE DISTRIBUTION   A distribution of the opponents' cards in a suit that gives the declarer less chance of making the contract.

VOID   A holding of no cards in a suit.

WINNER   A trick which either the declarer or the defender can win. A sure trick, or quick winner, is one that either side can take without giving up the lead. A slow winner is one that can be developed by giving up the lead.